Techniques for Coaching and Mentoring

Techniques for Coaching and Mentoring

David Megginson
David Clutterbuck

ELSEVIER
BUTTERWORTH
HEINEMANN

AMSTERDAM BOSTON HEIDELBERG LONDON NEW YORK OXFORD
PARIS SAN DIEGO SAN FRANCISCO SINGAPORE SYDNEY TOKYO

Elsevier Butterworth-Heinemann
Linacre House, Jordan Hill, Oxford OX2 8DP
30 Corporate Drive, Burlington, MA 01803

First published 2005

British Library Cataloguing in Publication Data
A catalogue record for this book is available from the British Library

Library of Congress Control Number: 2004116786

ISBN 0 7506 5287 X

For information on all Elsevier Butterworth-Heinemann publications
visit our website at http://books.elsevier.com

Typeset by Charon Tec Pvt. Ltd, Chennai, India
www.charontec.com
Printed and bound in Great Britain

Working together to grow
libraries in developing countries

www.elsevier.com | www.bookaid.org | www.sabre.org

ELSEVIER   BOOK AID
            International   Sabre Foundation

Contents

Foreword

This book has several purposes. It is designed to provide a resource for all those working in the field of one-to-one helping. It gives processes and tools (we use the term 'techniques') to do their job well. We also give vivid examples from within our own or our collaborators' experience to give context and point to the techniques described.

The book contributes to integrating the sub-fields of mentoring and coaching, as most of these techniques are appropriate to both, and we are not precious about definitions and pecking orders.

It also attempts to liberate the field from the comforting but ultimately oppressive thrall of various schools. If someone says to you, 'Are you a psychodynamic coach or a cognitive behavioural coach; an NLP mentor, or a TA mentor, or a psychosynthesis mentor?' this book encourages you to stand free of such commitments. It fortifies those who want to say, 'I choose how to go on in my one-to-one helping from a whole range of traditions and frameworks'. This book is for those who have learned one way or picked up a range of ways of doing the job, and want to extend that range.

In becoming the coaches and mentors we are today, the authors have worked in and learned from a multiplicity of schools of helping. This book seeks to distil our experience and to offer approaches that can be used by people like us with a range of experience who want to bring that full experience to bear onto the issues of the people we are helping. The risk of operating solely within one of the rich traditions that we have drawn upon is that you require the learner to define their issue in the terms of the discipline. We stand resolutely against such an approach – and in favour of defining the issue in the learner's own terms and finding the resources that will help them deal with this.

David Megginson
David Clutterbuck
Sheffield Hallam University
May 2004

Part 1

Introduction

What do you need in order to become a good coach or mentor: a life; a position; a qualification; a way of going on; techniques? Our answer to this question is, 'All of these'. Interestingly, given the focus of this book, we think that the least important of these resources for a coach or mentor is 'techniques'. However, most of the others in our list you will have acquired during the course of a life well lived. So all that many people need in order to become an excellent coach or mentor is the top-up of a range of techniques. You do need 'a way of going on' as well, and we will address that matter later in this introductory part of the book.

The aim of this volume is to provide the coach or mentor with a wider portfolio of techniques and approaches to helping others than would normally be gained from practical experience or attending a course. In compiling these techniques, we started with a fairly long list of situations, which we had met in our own coaching and mentoring activities, and added to these with the help of other experienced professionals in the field.

In due course, we were able to cluster these into a number of themes, which now make up the framework for the main body of this book (Part 2). These techniques are grouped into the following chapters:

1. Establishing and managing the coaching or mentoring relationship.
2. Setting goals.
3. Clarifying and understanding situations.
4. Building self-knowledge.
5. Understanding other people's behaviour.
6. Dealing with roadblocks.
7. Stimulating creative thinking.
8. Deciding what to do.
9. Committing to action.
10. Managing the learner's own behaviours.
11. Building wider networks of support, influence and learning.
12. Review and ending the coaching or mentoring relationship.
13. Building your own techniques.

We then drew upon our own experience and – in true coaching/mentoring style – approached a wide circle of other professionals to identify as many ways as possible of approaching each theme and the situations within it.

The clusters require a little more explanation. Taking each in turn:

1. *Establishing and managing the coaching or mentoring relationship*
   This cluster includes all the processes for setting up a coaching or mentoring relationship. These include getting to know each other, establishing the grounds for relationship success, creating and maintaining rapport and clarifying mutual expectations within the relationship.
2. *Setting goals*
   Issues here include raising horizons and visioning, assessing and choosing between options, and identifying gaps and needs to lead to a course of action. They also include identifying the goal that you really want.
3. *Clarifying and understanding situations*
   This involves helping people understand through metaphor, story and drama. There are techniques for mapping the context, and identifying the components of a situation. It includes developing both intellectual and emotional understanding.
4. *Building self-knowledge*
   In contrast to the previous chapter, which is externally focused, this one is about techniques that help the individual to look at themselves – for example, techniques that help people to identify and access personal values, to change belief sets, to bring stereotypes into the open and to understand their life and career.
5. *Understanding other people's behaviour*
   The focus turns external again, on to understanding others. We look at empathy, which is much neglected or disparaged in other texts, and then we explore bridging difference between the helper and learner, particularly within diversity programmes. We address stereotyping.
6. *Dealing with roadblocks*
   Issues here include identifying and recognising the nature of the roadblock, and the value of respecting the blocks. We also look at the alternative strategies of living with them or moving them, paying particular attention to addressing emotions in these processes.
7. *Stimulating creative thinking*
   Issues here include being live and dealing with internal conflicts that reduce creativity. Big assumptions, values and beliefs are explored and a technique is presented which helps people to articulate complex problems. Modelling situations is described and the place of a belief in being lucky is outlined.

8. *Deciding what to do*
   Coming to the point of what to do can be difficult for some people who are inclined to prevaricate. Techniques included here will help people make the decision that will unlock future commitment to action. We look at a spectrum from helping learners to do less to encouraging them to impel themselves into more action.
9. *Committing to action*
   The commitment following a decision is a crucial part of the work of coaches and mentors and involves alignment of head, heart and guts. Emotions, beliefs and assumptions play a part here as in so much of coaching and mentoring. We look at a means of calibrating commitment and thus increasing it and at how a sense of danger reduces it. We end the chapter with two perspectives on the place of personal development planning.
10. *Managing the learner's own behaviours*
    Issues here include helping learners to focus and attend to their issues and the depth approaches to enable individuals to take a strong grasp of their behaviour, particularly where they are embroiled in patterns or habits that are deeply ingrained.
11. *Building wider networks of support, influence and learning*
    We look at how the coach or mentor helps the learner to develop other resources upon which they can draw. This cluster also includes processes for maximising learning in the helping relationship.
12. *Ending the coaching or mentoring relationship*
    The main issue here is how the coach or mentor terminates the relationship, leaving the learner stronger for the intervention. Also here we explore the crucial part that review plays in maximising learning and preparing for a good closure.
13. *Some generic techniques*
    These are techniques that can be used across the stages implicit in the previous twelve clusters, for example, story telling and questioning. There are issues about managing the portfolio of techniques, keeping a record of these and ensuring that techniques that are used are focused firmly on the agenda of the learner.

What is a technique?

Techniques are related to other terms but also subtly different from them. They are similar to models, but in addition have a process for using the model attached to them. So 'thinking, feeling, willing' is a model, but our technique on this, called 'Head, heart and guts' in Part 2, Chapter 8, offers a process for using this model when dealing with roadblocks.

Techniques are similar to tools, but again have a process attached to them. Tools are devices that help us to talk about issues – the balloon and basket in Chapter 2 or the Russian dolls in Chapter 6. In making these into techniques we outline some key ideas about using the tool in practice, so that what starts as a dissociative way of creative thinking becomes a method for achieving a specific purpose.

Similarly, techniques are like processes, but whereas processes are relatively content free we describe the context that the process may be used in and the purposes that it might serve.

So, in summary, we define a technique as:

> A process to assist a mentee or coachee to address a specific purpose within a particular context as part of an ongoing development relationship

Coaching and/or mentoring

One of the problems practitioners in this field face is confusion of definitions. Particularly when describing professional interventions for executives, what one group describes as coaching, another would perceive as mentoring. It is not our task to be pedantic about this – what matters is clarity between the two partners in a developmental relationship about what is expected of them. However, our own view (and so far as we can tell, the majority view) is that:

- *Coaching* relates primarily to performance improvement (often over the short term) in a specific skills area. The goals, or at least the intermediate or sub-goals, are typically set with or at the suggestion of the coach. While the learner has primary ownership of the goal, the coach has primary ownership of the process. In most cases, coaching involves direct extrinsic feedback (i.e. the coach reports to the coachee what s/he has observed).
- *Mentoring* relates primarily to the identification and nurturing of potential for the whole person. It can be a long-term relationship, where the goals may change but are always set by the learner. The learner owns both the goals and the process. Feedback comes from within the mentee – the mentor helps them to develop insight and understanding through intrinsic observation (i.e. becoming more aware of their own experiences).

Much of the confusion arises because the skills of mentor and coach overlap to some extent. Elsewhere (Clutterbuck, 1998), one of the authors has identified four styles of coach: these can at their simplest be described as *tell, show, suggest* and *stimulate*. Coaches in stimulator style are behaving like a mentor – using their own experience to ask questions that lead learners to their own insights and conclusions, helping them to develop their own wisdom their own experience. But mentors also have a number of other roles to play, which are typically outside the coach's remit. They help the learner to build wider networks, from which to learn and influence; they act as sounding board and counsellor, responding to the individual's need for emotional support; and they act as adviser and, frequently, role model. Most of these behaviours and roles are not appropriate or relevant for coaching – for example, the professional psychologist, who has no experience of being at the top of a business, would not want to be a role model or sounding board on strategy for a chief executive. Such helpers, with their depth of professional understanding, can often be a much better source of help in focusing on specific behavioural performance improvements than the elder statesman coach who has been there and done it.

Our intention with this book has been neither to contribute to the confusion about what is and isn't coaching or mentoring; nor to impose our own views of the distinctions between the two roles. A more productive approach, we feel, is to view coaching, mentoring, counselling and other developmental functions as occupying relatively flexible areas of *developmental space*. In early work by Clutterbuck (*Everyone Needs a Mentor*, 2nd edition, CIPD, London, 1992), two dimensions were identified. Directiveness refers to where the power lies in the relationship and how it is managed, while the need dimension refers to whether the relationship focuses primarily on helping the learner with rational or emotional issues. Each quadrant provided a base camp for a particular developmental style or role.

More recently, we have begun to identify other possible dimensions to developmental space. Three candidates are represented in the diagram below.

Doing is about achieving change in skills or performance; *becoming* about changing one's ambitions, perspectives and sense of identity.

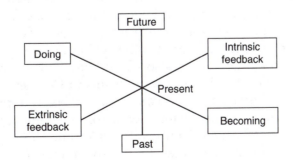

Extrinsic and intrinsic feedback relate to who observes, analyses, interprets and owns an experience.

Future, *present* and *past* relate to the chronology of change. It can be (and has been) argued that counselling is mainly about dealing with the past, coaching about the present and mentoring about the future. This is overly simplistic, to say the least, but there is at least a grain of truth in the concept.

Our assertion is that all developmental relationships, however and by whomsoever they are defined, exist in multidimensional developmental space. Establishing the minutiae of difference between developmental roles, or arguing over terminology is of much less significance than understanding where each role exists within developmental space – where its heartland lies and which territories it is able to expand into, as and when the need arises.

So our challenge to the reader is that you should:

- determine the contours of the developmental space in which you operate or wish to operate;
- call it what you like (but remember you have to be able to communicate the meaning to those people with whom you work and, in the case of the professional coach or mentor, to whoever pays the bill)
- be consistent with your own definition
- be aware of the role boundaries and the boundaries of your own competence

In a recent study of competencies for mentors (*The Situational Mentor*, Clutterbuck and Lane, Gower, Aldershot, 2004), one of us proposed that a fundamental developmental skill was balancing boundary management, while exhibiting a high level of flexibility in response. Part of the motivation in producing this book is a perception that response flexibility comes from having a wide portfolio of techniques, concepts and models to call upon as needed.

The words we use most frequently in this book to describe the protagonists are *coach* or *mentor* for the helper and *mentee* or *coachee* for the person helped. We often use both together, but if a technique seems particularly useful in one or the other approach, we just use the one. This is particularly the case when the author of the technique is one of our contributors and comes from one tradition or the other. Other terms we use are *helper* and *helpee* or *helped*. One of us also really likes Myles Downey's term *player* for the helpee. He makes a case for this in Downey, 2004, but the other author was not so keen on this, so it has not been adopted as standard here. Eric Parsloe of the Oxford School of Coaching and Mentoring advocates the use of the hybrid term *coach-mentor*, and although we can see good arguments for this on occasion, it also smooths over differences, which, we believe, are worth retaining. We also like the term *learner* for the person being helped, but it has the disadvantage of suggesting that only one party to the relationship is learning and this flies in the face of both good practice and lived experience. Occasionally we use the term *client* for the person being helped, though we acknowledge that this fits better with the relationships of professional, paid coaches than it does with people working as volunteers or working for the same organisation as the person they are helping.

The pros and cons of techniques

This book is designed to offer the reader a range of interventions that they can employ when working one-to-one with others. Our purpose is to enlarge the range of techniques that you can use in this important work of helping, and thus make it more effective. So, the rationale for the publication is that:

- users will be able to be more specifically helpful than they otherwise would, in a wider range of situations than before;
- they will feel more able to address intractable situations or reluctant learners knowing that they have a way of going on in these situations;
- they will, consequently, feel less anxious and more at peace in making their intervention, thus enabling the learner the better to benefit from it.

Our writing this book has the additional purpose of offering those helping with the training and development of mentors and coaches a collection of techniques that they can use in their own training and development efforts.

Some readers may feel a twinge of disquiet at reading these purposes. We, the authors, share this feeling, and we discuss potential sources of the concern here to act as a caution against inappropriate use.

The concerns about a manual of this kind are as follows:

- It can lead to helping-by-numbers, where the user does not have the knowledge or skill to use the technique appropriately.
- In particular, a technique may come from a particular framework for development and to be used appropriately it must be employed within the context of that framework. By taking one of the techniques from this book and using it in isolation, readers run the risk of stripping away the context that gives it meaning.
- The best tools are those that are invented on the spur of the moment. Even frameworks like gestalt therapy and NLP were invented by founders who themselves valued spontaneity and creating unique

solutions whenever the need arose (Perls, 1971; Bandler and Grinder, 1975).

- Some techniques, and NLP is particularly prone to this, can be used for illegitimate purposes – a point we explore later in this chapter.
- Collections of techniques, like the competency frameworks they are often associated with, are essentially atomistic. They work by breaking a complex task into simple components. There is no guarantee that such a procedure enables one to reconstruct the whole from the parts.

In assembling this book we have adopted a number of strategies for minimizing the downside of the points listed above and maximizing the benefits cited earlier. These strategies are as follows:

- We have only used techniques that we, or our contributors, have used in practice, usually on multiple occasions. So these processes have a ring of truth about them. They have all been tested in hard professional practice with demanding clients.
- We are advocating a model of mentoring and coaching that might be described as the British Eclectic model. This stance recognizes that there are some powerful meta-models out there which frame some coaching and mentoring practices, such as psychoanalysis (Lee, 2003) or NLP (McDermott and Jago, 2001). Nonetheless, we argue that the risk of being a coach, who offers a solution in search of a problem, is greater with strong models than it is with looser, more eclectic approaches.
- Given the potential downside of collections of techniques, we hold that it is better to have lots of techniques than only a few. If you only have a hammer then you can only deal with nails; we seek to provide screwdrivers, chisels and files but also directories for good builders, alternative ways of hanging pictures on walls, and considering whether free-standing sculptures might look better than pictures anyway.
- These techniques are also of use to a wide range of coaching and mentoring clients, for a multiplicity of purposes, and are useable by a range of different practitioners. If you have particular clients or specific foci, or if you brand yourself in a way that excludes certain types of intervention, then the discussion in this introductory part of the text outlining the techniques and how they fit together will enable you to focus your search for inspiration within this compendium.
- Helping to crystallize what we do into a series of techniques can make it explicit both to ourselves and to those we help. This in itself can lead to a freer more equal negotiation of what to do and how to do it in the relationship.

NLP, coaching techniques and speed-seduction

As suggested above there are some approaches that are more amenable to manipulation and unprofessional (or downright illegitimate) use than others. One of the most popular and yet widely criticized such techniques is NLP or Neuro-Linguistic Programming.

A short article in *Observer Magazine* p. 10, 8th February 2004 demonstrates a wholly manipulative use of NLP. The *What's the Word?* feature talked about 'sarging', a verb meaning 'intending to speed-seduce'.

'Pick-up Artists' (PUAs) are men who practise, study and fine-tune techniques for speed seduction, a method of sexual acquisition first espoused by a named author who we do not intend to publicize, who is the most noted 'Pick-up Guru' (PUG), incorporating (as the article reports) the hypnosis-like 'tricks' of neuro-linguistic programming .... A PUA refers to his combined seduction skills and resources as his 'toolbox' and to any entranced look on a female face as 'doggy dinner bowl'. He will use negs (negative remarks to break a seducee's indifference), kino (touching methods), language-mirroring and ambiguity ('below me' suggests 'blow me').

This is enough to give you the gist of this contemptible behaviour. What is the relevance of the article to the, surely, more morally desirable issue of coaching and mentoring techniques? Well, if we are doing things *to* others then, however we dress it up, it has resonance of the kind of manipulation presented in the Observer article.

So if we are to use techniques at all, then, it seems to us, a minimum of two design requirements should be in place. First, the coach should use the technique openly and in consultation with the coachee; and secondly, the technique's intended effects should be discussed and agreed before embarking on it. There is no justification for magical manipulation and trickery in the work of a mentor or coach. However, this injunction from us does not entirely deal with the issue. We are sure that many of the pioneers and innovators of NLP had nothing but the highest values and concerns for humankind. It did not stop their work being abused by the despicable PUGs and their abject and deluded PUAs. Gas chambers, like NLP techniques, are morally neutral. It depends on how you use them. Taking these considerations into account we have eschewed offering NLP techniques that have the potential to be used manipulatively and have focused instead on frameworks and processes that work best with the wholehearted and informed consent of both parties. Of course, there are many users of NLP techniques who do so ethically and with appropriate provisos and concern for the technique to be used democratically. A notable example of this approach to NLP in coaching is McLeod (2003) (see Part 3).

Relationship to competency models

This book is timely, given the current exponential growth in mentoring and coaching. It is however, not timely in that it is being completed shortly before the European Mentoring and Coaching Council comes out with its model of competencies. The Chartered Institute of Personnel and Development is currently producing a Buyers' Guide to Coaching and Mentoring, which, again, will seek to spell out the dimensions of the field, and is considering the development of its own framework of competencies. The authors have been centrally engaged with both these initiatives and we have integrated what we know about the emerging shape of this work into our frameworks; however, there may be further fine-tuning to do in subsequent editions.

A way of going on

Techniques are all very well; in fact they are what gives variety and point to our helping sessions. However, they need some glue or substrate – something to link them together into a coherent process. Otherwise recipients of our help are going to have a sense of being worked over – first he tried this, then that, then something else. By holding the reflective space (Clutterbuck and Megginson, 1999, pp. 8–10) the helper makes it safe for the player to explore and skilled coaches and mentors encourage the people they are helping to make as many choices themselves about how to work and what to work on. Indeed some authorities, such as Downey (2004), argue that the player should make the entire running in what they see as a self-directed process. Others, such as Clutterbuck (1998), argue that there is a range of techniques, from non-directive to directive, that can be used depending upon the readiness of the learner.

We have long felt in training mentors that it is best for each mentor to develop their own process (Clutterbuck and Megginson, 1999, pp. 149–50). And in either coaching or mentoring it seems crucial that we have 'a way of going on' that extends beyond the end of one activity and starts before the beginning of the next. To use a musical analogy we need to think of the long line that the music is taking, rather than just concentrating on the current brief phrase. It is interesting to note that the *i-coach academy* (see Part 3 for further details) spends the first half of their 2-year part time Masters programme helping participants to identify just such a process. There are dangers in this approach too, of course. The Masters students at Sheffield Hallam University (see Part 3 again) thought that this too was rather a restrictive approach, but, if nothing else, it highlights the need for deep thought about how you are going to work as a helper.

Using this book

This book can be used in a number of ways:

● As general preparation – thinking through a range of techniques that you might be faced with in the future and seeing the techniques offered here as extending the range of the possible.
● As specific preparation – if you feel stuck with a particular client, use the contents and index and flick through the chapters as a means of finding something that may help to unlock possibility for the client.
● As an agenda for a course on coaching or mentoring where the various techniques for different stages can be used as a source for practice. In preparing drafts of this book, we have found that it is energizing for participants to choose which activities from a particular chapter they want to practice. Now you have all the chapters in your hand, you could also allow participants to choose which chapters they wish to focus upon.

When you are trying out a technique for the first time, it makes sense before using it with someone else to work through it on your own. You may want to use some of the 107 questions in Chapter 13, to prompt you to think about the issue. Next, if you have the opportunity, try it out with colleagues and friends. They (if you are fortunate) will be candid in telling you what worked or didn't work for them. It is well to remember that what doesn't work for one person may well be helpful for another, but all the time you are building up case experience in addition to the cases that we include throughout this book. All our cases, incidentally, are based on real experience, with only circumstantial details changed to protect the identity of the learner.

When you use a technique for the first time, stick fairly closely to the brief. Even if you cannot see the purpose of some part of the process, give it a try and let experience be a teacher. Of course, if you are sure that something is not relevant or desirable in your case then start without it. Even here, ask yourself the question 'What function did that part of the technique have, and how could this function be met without it?' Once you have your own case experience, then adapt like mad, and make it your own. There is a risk of over-specifying when first introducing a technique – the more detail, the more it becomes a mere procedure, so, at all times, it is crucial to maintain client focus and stay on their agenda. Setting up and exploring buy-in are a crucial part of using any technique.

Contributors and acknowledgements

There have been many people, who have contributed to the thinking behind, and the words in, this book, and we would like to thank them all. We apologize to any whom we may have inadvertently omitted in the lists below.

We are particularly grateful to the following, who have contributed to the various chapters (numbered) with a technique of their own.

(1) Kate Hopkinson
(2) Joyce Russell and Robert Smith
(3) Steve O'Shaughnessy and Sharon Collins
(3) Dianne Hawken
(4) Mari Watson
(4) Sandra Henson
(4) Lloyd Denton
(4) Julie Allan
(5) Eileen Murphy
(5) Amarjeet Rebolo
(5) Caroline Beery and Maria Jicheva
(5) Zulfi Hussein
(6) Barbara Jakob
(6) Marlene Spero
(7) Mike Turner
(7) Richard Hale
(7) Kate Hopkinson
(7 & 8) Vivien Whitaker
(9) Phil Donnison
(9) Gillian Hill
(9) Linda Phipps
(10) Julian Lippi
(11 & 12) Peter Matthews.

Others who have given generously of their ideas include:

Bob Garvey, Diane Lennan, Dolores Sarayon, Eckard König, Elizabeth Gordon Duffy, Gil Schwenk, Gill Lewis, Gurbinder Bahra, Jan Kingsley, Jens Maier, Kate Howsley, Kate Kennett, Lis Merrick, Maíre Shelly, Mike van Oudtshoorn, Paul O'Donovan Rossa, Paul Stokes, Peter Bluckert, Peter English, Richard Field, Ruth Garrett-Harris, Terry Gibson, Theo Groot, Ian Martin and Tom Cox.

We would like to reserve special thanks for Jenny Sweeney and Terry Gibson, without whose massive support at crucial times in bringing this project to completion, you would not be reading this book now.

References

Bandler, R. and Grinder, J. (1975). *The Structure of Magic*. Palo Alto, CA: Science & Behavior Books.

Clutterbuck, D. (1998). *Learning Alliances*. London: CIPD.

Clutterbuck, D. and Megginson, D. (1999). *Mentoring Executives and Directors*. Oxford: Butterworth-Heinemann.

Downey, M. (2004). *Effective Coaching*, 2nd edn. London: Texere.

Lee, G. (2003). *Leadership Coaching*. London: CIPD.

McDermott, I. and Jago, W. (2001). *The NLP Coach*. London: Piatkus.

McLeod, A. (2003). *Performance Coaching: A Handbook for Managers, H. R. Professionals and Coaches*. Bancyfelin, Carmarthen: Crown House.

Perls, F. (1971). *Gestalt Therapy Verbatim*. New York: Bantam.

Part 2

The Techniques

This Part represents the bulk of the book and it is organized into the thirteen chapters listed below.

1. Establishing and managing the coaching or mentoring relationship.
2. Setting goals.
3. Clarifying and understanding situations.
4. Building self-knowledge.
5. Understanding other people's behaviour.
6. Dealing with roadblocks.
7. Stimulating creative thinking.
8. Deciding what to do.
9. Committing to action.
10. Managing the learner's own behaviour.
11. Building wider networks of support, influence and learning.
12. Review and ending the coaching or mentoring relationship.
13. Building your own techniques.

The titles of the chapters should be treated only as approximate themes, because we experienced a great deal of overlap in the potential use of techniques within different themes. As suggested in Chapter 13, we encourage you to develop your own library of techniques, and to organize these in whatever way best serves your own purposes. If you use a strong model, such as GROW, then it might make sense to have just four themes – Goals, Reality, Outcomes and Will (or Wrap-up).

At the start of each chapter there is an introduction which:

- presents general ideas about the theme embraced in the chapter,
- outlines the principle by which the techniques have been sequenced,
- specifies the various sections (if any) into which the chapter has been divided, and
- introduces and names the activities included.

The body of each chapter deals with the techniques, with brief introductions to sections. Otherwise, technique follows technique, and, because they vary considerably in length, each technique's title is in bold (whereas subheadings are italicized and section titles are in bold and underlined). Case studies are included in a great many of the longer techniques, and these are typically named after the protagonist(s) involved. These names have been altered to protect the identity of the people involved.

Chapter 1

Establishing and managing the relationship

Introduction

This first chapter is a long one as there are lots of things to do if you are to get a coaching or mentoring relationship off to a good start. We have divided the chapter into four sections:

- Getting to know each other.
- Establishing the grounds for relationship success.
- Rapport.
- Setting expectations.

In each section we include a brief introduction to the topic and we deal with two or more techniques. In this chapter, we have only one technique written by one of our co-authors, and we are grateful to Kate Hopkinson for her challenging critique of attempts to reduce rapport to a question of mere technique.

Getting to know each other

People come to coaching or mentoring relationships for a wide variety of reasons and in many different contexts. But a common factor is that the relationship is unlikely to proceed very far – or at least, is unlikely to produce substantial positive results – if there is not initial rapport.

Mutual consent, a willingness to participate in the relationship, is normally seen as an essential precursor to effective *relationships* in both coaching and mentoring. There are some circumstances, where one party or the other may be an unwilling partner or an unaware partner (for example, the direct report, where the person does not want to be coached; or where the person is selected as mentee by someone more senior, who takes a proactive interest in their development, without specifically revealing a mentoring intent). The former is not a positive relationship; the latter may not be a relationship at all in the normal meaning of the term.

Equally important as rapport, in our experience, may be having a broad sense of purpose – a mutual understanding of what the relationship is about, even if there is not a fixed, preset goal to achieve. Even a laissez-faire friendship can have an element of being available, of being able to provide practical or psychosocial support from time to time. Figure 1.1 indicates the value of a combination of rapport and goal clarity. Relationships with low rapport but high clarity can still deliver results in terms of performance, learning or both together. Relationships with low clarity but high rapport can be enjoyable, but are likely to deliver less personal change. Relationships high in both can be argued to be the most rewarding and successful, in terms of measurable outcomes. Where both rapport and goal clarity are low, little can reasonably be expected.

Figure 1.1   Relationship between goal clarity and rapport in mentoring. (Reproduced with permission from *Mentoring and Diversity*, by Clutterbuck and Ragins.)

Building the relationship requires skill, patience (often a skill itself) and an adaptive portfolio of techniques. In this section, we explore some practical ways of:

- getting to know each other,
- creating the environment for rapport, and
- engaging the coachee/mentee in the rapport-building process.

Getting to know you (1) Conversation ladder

There is a well-known technique of questioning that we learned from industrialist and executive coach Richard Field, and which we call 'Conversation ladder'. It derives from many self-help models, including Dale Carnegie, where it is called the conversation stack. There are two principles at work in this stack. One is to ask a set of questions about topics of central concern to people, which they will love talking about. The second is to retain in memory the sequence (the steps on the ladder), using imagery to do it.

All the areas are about the person themselves. What other topic can compete with these, in terms of interest, or indeed its capacity for developing rapport? A typical list of steps on the ladder might be as follows:

- Their name and its significance to them
- Family of origin
- Home and current family
- Education
- Work
- Successes
- Difficulties
- Interests
- Dreams/aspirations.

If you ask someone questions about each of these then you will build a reputation for being a very fine listener. There is a story about Victoria, at the end of her reign, thinking back over the prime ministers she had met, and saying, 'After an evening with Mr Gladstone, you are convinced that he is the cleverest person in England; after an evening with Mr Disraeli I felt that *I* was the cleverest person in England'. You can guess who was her favourite prime minister, and you can imagine him using a conversation ladder something like this, with one or two extra questions like, 'Which is the most difficult country to rule, and why? What problems do you have with your cousins?'

The second part of the technique uses the approach, popularized by many books on improving your memory, of having a set of vivid images of the steps on your ladder to help you remember the sequence. So, for example, the sequence on page 19 can be retained by having in mind the following:

- A brass nameplate on a purple door.
- Inside, a woman changing a nappy on the person you are getting to know.
- Zooming out to the house again.
- A scholar slouching to school.
- The same scholar sitting behind a huge desk.
- Through the window a snow covered peak with a tiny figure planting a flag in the top of it.
- An avalanche undermining the figure's position.
- And a beautiful garden clinging to the slopes.
- As the figure looks at the garden they fly off the mountain and sail towards a pass between two peaks.

Use whatever images you wish to build your own ladder. The images are just to remind you to explore a range of areas.

Getting to know you (2)

It is not unusual for a coach or mentor to encounter someone who likes to maintain a high wall around themselves, protecting their privacy to the extent that it is hard for others to get to know them. Of course, it is possible to have a relationship with such a person, perhaps on a very amicable and even relaxed basis, but the relationship will lack depth and richness.

The reasons why some people are unwilling and/or unable to share about themselves are many, ranging from the clinical (e.g. Asperger's syndrome) to a fear of being exposed. It is not normally the coach/mentor's role to provide therapeutic counselling in such situations, even if he or she is qualified to do so. The dilemma is often one of reconciling the demand of the relationship for greater openness and rapport, with the desire of the individual not to venture into personal areas.

Circles of disclosure

In this simple technique, the coach or mentor explains that no part of our life is completely separate from the others. What happens to us at work influences our behaviour at home – for example, how tired and/or irritable we are in the evening, whether we have the mental energy to go out and do something active or just want to vegetate. Similarly, what happens to us at home can have an impact on how well we focus on the job at work.

Starting on relatively safe ground, the coach/mentor helps the learner identify a number of dimensions of work which are relevant – for example, doing routine tasks on one's own, working as part of the team, attending cross-team meetings. She or he then draws a circle and labels it *Performance*, or *Personal Achievement*, or whatever is acceptable to the learner. The edge of the circle is the *Border of Disclosure* – the boundary between the private and the public. If each of the dimensions previously discussed is another circle, how much of it lies within the main circle – all, some, or none?

The visual image takes the discussion from the emotional to the intellectual, which is usually much less threatening. As the learner becomes comfortable with discussing, say, how much openness is appropriate for a situation with which they feel comfortable, they can gradually be helped to identify other circles. As well as intersecting the main circle, some of these additional circles will intersect or encompass each other. Discussing the relationship between these circles puts distance between the issues and the emotions surrounding them. At the same time, however, it opens up a panoply of relatively safe routes in to more personal topics. (See Miranda's case study below.)

Another version of this technique (see Peter's case study on page 23) views the border as being between current and potential capability.

Where and how to use circles of disclosure

This technique can be used anywhere, where there are issues that the individual finds it difficult to address, or does not accept that certain issues are relevant to the coaching or mentoring relationship. It is useful to remember that, ultimately, the decision on what to disclose and what is relevant belongs to them, not to the coach or mentor.

Case study   **Miranda**

Miranda is an experienced professional in the client services function of an IT provider company. Her role requires her to maintain good relationships both with the customers and with the engineers, who design and implement technical solutions to customers' problems. At the time in question, she had come into conflict with several of her internal colleagues and this had come to the attention of her manager. When he tried to address the issue, she dismissed the problem, saying only that it was a temporary matter and she'd sort it out.

(Continued)

And so she did. She made a point of seeking out the colleagues in question and smoothing things over with them.

All was well, until 6 months later, when the same problem recurred. This time, the manager, an experienced coach, set aside time to discuss matters with her in detail. Clearly, something was causing the dysfunctional behaviour; would she like to talk about it? No, she wouldn't. It was a personal matter, nothing to do with work, and would be resolved shortly again.

The manager accepted that there were boundaries of disclosure, but explained that they should nonetheless discuss how she might better manage her behaviour towards colleagues while the issue outside of work was affecting her. Would it be appropriate for her to reveal to colleagues that she was under stress and would appreciate some tolerance from them for a while? After some thought, she agreed it would – but only to those who needed to know.

Would it be appropriate to talk about sources of help within the company? 'But it's not the company's problem!' Nonetheless, explained the manager, anything that affected work performance was an interest of the company and there were specific resources to help with a wide range of problems. Tentatively, she drew a small circle across the main circle rim. She would listen to what was available, she explained, but she didn't want to go into detail about her personal life.

The coach started to explain what counselling services were available. When he talked about supporting carers, Miranda was unable to hide her interest. A few sensitive questions later, she was explaining in detail about her difficulties managing the care of her mother, who, although only in her sixties, was suffering severely from Alzheimer's disease. The emotional trauma of watching the decay of someone she loved had been bad enough; especially as she felt guilty at pursuing her own career, so not having spent much time with her mother. Indeed, it was this feeling of guilt, she admitted, that was the main reason behind her reluctance to discuss the matter – she felt ashamed of her neglect.

There was also a lot of travel involved at weekends, because her mother lived 100 miles away. Just as she thought she had come to terms with this practical and emotional upheaval in her life, and was beginning to cope, a further problem arose. With her mother's savings exhausted, the financial burden of care fell on Miranda's shoulders.

Although the coach couldn't solve these problems for her, he was able to direct her to support services that eased the burden to some extent. He also put her in touch with a colleague in another department, who had been through a similar experience and would be willing to talk about it. Miranda recognized that this was exactly the kind of confidante that she wanted. Exchanging experiences with this person helped her overcome much of the guilt feeling and prepared her for other effects of her mother's deterioration as it progressed. In due course, she also opened up to her colleagues and found them highly supportive.

Case study   Peter

Peter is a middle-aged manager, who has come up the ladder 'the hard way.' He left school at 16, spent a time as an apprentice and had become a team leader by the time his talent for getting things done was noticed. His career was characterized by taking on difficult tasks and persuading others to collaborate in making them happen. He was well respected within the company as someone who understood both the employee perspective and the business need. He also had a reputation for showing little tolerance for theoretical discussion and was prone to come into conflict with departments such as strategic planning, which he would berate for being too 'airy fairy'.

The CEO and the HR director both recognized Peter's talent for dealing with people in most other contexts and saw him as a potential board member if he could add to his instinctive grasp of business situations a more analytical approach. However, Peter strongly resisted being put in situations that demanded deep analysis. He did attend an intensive 2-week strategic leadership programme at a leading business school, under some pressure, but it was clear he did not enjoy it. Yet he remained highly ambitious.

The issue was raised in Peter's annual appraisal and the suggestion made that he use an external coach. He agreed with some reluctance and made it clear at the meeting that all he needed was some specific skills development in analytical techniques.

The coach got him to draw a circle, which Peter agreed to describe as *What I need to make director*. Inside the circle were to be the attributes he had now; outside, those that he need to develop more fully. The coach started with an uncontentious issue, track record on delivery. Peter decided that he was 80 per cent inside the circle on this issue.

The coach then drew out other areas of capability that might be expected of a director, such as being a good communicator and being a role model for the values of the organization. From the latter, he suggested they examine how Peter saw himself as a role model for learning. This led to an analysis of what learning Peter had undertaken during his career and what kind of things he felt most and least comfortable learning. One key statement was 'I don't need all that intellectual stuff'.

The coach used that statement to explore what Peter meant by 'intellectual'. Peter used a lot of dismissive phrases and words, such as airy fairy and half-baked. The coach asked him if he felt the same about intellect in the sense of good reasoning – 'That's what I call common sense' was the reply.

'But is common sense enough? Don't you also need clear thinking and accurate contextual knowledge?'

'Of course.'

'So what is it you found most and least valuable about the leadership course? When did you feel in "flow" and when did you find it tough going?'

(Continued)

By gradually chipping at the edges, the coach elicited that Peter felt least comfortable when he was trying to hold his own in a discussion with quick-thinking, highly intelligent younger people. He eventually admitted to feeling intimidated and then, finally, that he had been devastated some years before by the results of a battery of psychometric tests he had undergone. One result, in particular, stuck in his consciousness – that he did not have a particularly high IQ. This admission opened the floodgates to a rush of self-recriminations about his failure to go to university and the inferiority he sometimes felt in the company of people who had – especially if they had advanced degrees or had gone to the 'best' universities.

Using the circle diagram, the coach helped Peter consider how much of a disadvantage this really was. He had demonstrated over the years that he was able to function at a high level by making use of the talents of brighter people around him – indeed, the identification, recruitment and motivation of these people was a key strength for him. The circle he needed to address was how he made himself even more effective in this rare and important capability by adding basic skills of analysis. He needed not to become a statistician, but simply to have sufficient know-how to ask the right questions and direct how he wanted the data presented to him.

Once he had accepted that it didn't matter whether he had a high IQ or not – that he could still be very effective in his current role and the director's role he aspired to – Peter decided that the analytical skills requirement was 70 per cent outside of the *What I need to make director* circle. The coach then helped him to plan a development approach, involving both self-study and just-in-time discussion. With the fear and self-doubt removed he was able to concentrate on learning the principles and was soon sufficiently confident to challenge data in a more rigorous manner.

The zone of discomfort

The best learning often takes place at the edge of what is known and accepted. Another simple approach to lowering the bar of what can be discussed and creating openness is to build into the 'contract' that the learner agrees you will take them, at least once each time you meet, into the zone of discomfort. Indeed, this can be a useful measure of how meaningful the relationship is.

Another phrase for this is 'Expanding the envelope'. Raj Persaud (2001) makes the point in his book *Keeping Sane* that we can either adapt ourselves to our environment to avoid challenge, or we can adapt ourselves so that we can become more adaptable. This adaptation is not in the sense of being compliant, but rather in terms of embracing a wider range of phenomena. Persaud uses the example of a person who is phobic about going to the upper floors of buildings, and who developed elaborate routines for avoiding having to do so:

> This person was clearly not trying to change to become more adaptable; instead her motivation was to adapt her situation to herself as she was .... Aiming to adapt to whatever situation you find yourself in is much harder at the time, and only pays dividends later.... But despite the difficulties, it is much more healthy to aspire to adaptability (Persaud, 2001, p. 116).

Establishing the grounds for relationship success

Many textbooks on mentoring recommend some form of contract between mentor and mentee. Both the authors of this book have serious reservations about introducing bureaucratic procedures into what is intended to be a relatively informal relationship. But the principle of agreeing and clarifying ground rules for the relationship does seem sound, both in theory and practice – the partners need to understand what each expects of the other, if they are to play their full part in the relationship.

The same basic principle applies within coaching. The coaching session will have greater impact if the coachee is a consenting partner, who takes an active role in making the coaching process work. He or she can only do this with clarity of expectation.

The world's best and worst

Sometimes, it is easier to identify behaviours and outcomes you want by beginning with those that you don't want. The coach/mentor and the learner each prepares a descriptive list for the coach/mentor and coachee/mentee from hell. In particular:

● What attitudes would they show?
● What behaviours would they exhibit?
● What would they *not* do?
● What kind of things would they say?
● What kind of things would they *not* say?

Characteristics of the coach/mentor from hell might include:

● always talking, never listening,
● arrogance,
● overfamiliarity,
● constantly postponing meetings.

Characteristics of the coachee/mentee from hell will typically be very similar.

The two parties exchange their lists and compare. Not only does the resulting discussion help to generate rapport, it also opens up specific concerns and fears about the relationship. Together, they extract themes that are appropriate for defining the positive behaviours each should expect of the other.

Next, the coach/mentor moves the conversation away from the relationship, to examine the context in which it will operate. She or he uses questions such as:

- What would undermine our relationship, or prevent it from working as well as it should?
- How will we make sure we don't fall into any of these traps?

The learning contract

Whether or not you use the above activity, at the start of any coaching or mentoring relationship it can be helpful to develop a joint contract for learning in order to:

- begin thinking through helper and helpee expectations of each other,
- identify any issues or concerns.

The method

1. Ask the learner why they think a contract is needed. Typical responses may be:
   - to clarify expectations about outcomes and behaviours;
   - to provide a baseline to measure progress;
   - to establish the boundaries of the relationship;
   - to establish who is responsible for what in managing the relationship.
2. Ask what they would expect/like to be in the contract and why. Encourage them to draw up a list of items to include, under two headings:
   - formal, to be written down;
   - informal, simply to be discussed so both parties share the same understanding.

Compare notes and discuss any differences of view. It is worth remembering that people want/need different levels of formality in the coaching/mentoring contract. Anything the mentee/coachee declares off limits may well be a key subject for discussion, once trust is established.

Issues to consider in the coaching or mentoring contract

The minimum requirement is that helper and helpee should discuss the issues of relationship purpose and relationship management sufficiently to acquire a shared understanding of them. The most common topics for this discussion are covered in the list below:

- What do we expect to learn from each other?
- What are our responsibilities towards each other? What are the limits?
- What responsibilities do we owe to others (e.g.: line managers; peers; HR function) as a result of this relationship?
- Where and how often shall we meet? For how long?
- What limits (if any) are there on confidentiality?
- When and how shall we check if this relationship is right for both of us?
- How happy are you for me to challenge and confront you?
- How do you feel about receiving blunt feedback from me?
- Do you feel you can be really open with me? If not, what makes you reticent?
- Is there anything either of us definitely does not want to talk about?
- Are we agreed that openness and trust are essential? How will we ensure they happen?
- Are we both willing to give honest and timely feedback (e.g. to be a critical friend)?
- What are we prepared to tell others about our discussions?
- How formal or informal do we want our meetings to be?
- How will we measure progress?
- How will we manage the various transitions especially at the end of the formal relationship?
- To what extent are we prepared to share networks?
- When and how shall we review the relationship?
- How will we celebrate achievements?

Like purpose, the 'contract' terms will evolve with the relationship. It is commonplace for one party or both to place quite narrow limits on how far the pair will delve into non-work issues, for example. Yet, as trust develops, the boundaries on discussion tend to soften or disappear completely.

If the relationship does not work out (even in the best of schemes, the chemistry may simply not be right), there has to be a mechanism for confronting the issue. Neither mentor nor mentee may be willing to say, 'Look, this isn't working, is it?,' for fear of embarrassment, letting the other person down, or even of retribution. The concept of 'no-fault divorce' is helpful here. Essentially, mentor and mentee are expected to engage in a discussion about whether they are suited to each other, after the first two or three meetings, at the latest. Both sides need to understand the importance of responding honestly and openly, and that it is better to deal with the issues now, when relatively little face will be lost by admitting the relationship will not work, than to be locked into a relationship which neither will find fulfilling.

The fact that a relationship did not gel at one point in the learner's progress does not mean that the same mentor will not have potential as a helper for the mentee in the future. Where the mismatch concerns style or relevance of experience (as opposed to trust), there is often a possibility of reinstating it at a later date. The case study in the box below illustrates just such a situation.

Case study   The reluctant mentee

John and Roger were assigned to each other under a graduate entry scheme in a large UK-based multinational. This was John's first job after university and he was having trouble adapting to the very different lifestyle in an organization. John found Roger, who was head of another department of 200 people, to be unsympathetic, overcritical and overwhelming.

John spoke to the personnel department about his reservations. A few days later he received a note from Roger suggesting four names of other, more junior managers he should contact, to choose his own mentor. He hit it off so well with Mary, the first on the list, that he didn't talk to any of the others.

Two years later, he had outgrown Mary's help and felt he was making a useful contribution to the company. He applied to join a high-profile project team, only to be dismayed when he discovered that Roger was on the selection panel.

The interview was every bit as tough as he expected, but, to his surprise, he enjoyed the experience. Even more to his surprise, Roger recommended his inclusion on the team. After working with Roger for a few months, John realized that he had matured to the point where Roger's challenging style was exactly what he needed. When the project ended, the two became mentor and mentee without anyone raising the subject. 'It just seemed the natural thing to do,' said John.

Among the most obvious clues as to whether a relationship is working is whether and how often people meet. There are, of course, no hard and fast rules about this, but a good guideline is that the pair should meet formally sufficiently often to create a real relationship, yet not so often that they develop dependency.

Rapport

What you feel passionate about

One of the most direct ways to gain an insight into someone else's values is to exchange information on what you both feel passionate about.

Although people often hesitate initially at being asked about such matters, they usually soon respond with enthusiasm, revealing aspects of their personality and interests that might otherwise be hidden. Themes might cover both work and non-work issues, but they all emphasize positive and enthusiastic elements of the individual's persona. The effective coach or mentor can often use these insights as anchors for other issues about which the learner feels less enthusiastic.

Creating the physical environment for rapport

It's obvious that some meeting environments are more conducive to reflective dialogue than others. But coaches and mentors are often caught out if they do not discuss openly with the learner where they should meet. In one case, the mentors deliberately chose to meet with shop floor supervisors in a 'neutral' office – not their own, because that would be seen as their space; not the supervisor's because that might seem threatening, because it was too noisy and too prone to interruption. It was only after some months that one of the mentors asked if meeting in the office of another manager, who was out for the day, was OK. 'No,' was the reply. The supervisor was acutely aware that he was not dressed appropriately for an office environment and was concerned he would leave oil stains on the carpet or the easy-chairs. The meetings shifted to an ante-room in the staff restaurant.

Some questions to help establish the environment to meet in:

- How shut off from the world do we want to be?
- How important is daylight?
- Do we need space to spread papers?
- What's the right balance between being relaxed and business-like?
- Where do you normally feel most at ease?
- What kind of environment makes you feel uncomfortable? Threatened?
- Do you prefer to work across a table, or without anything between us?
- How comfortable do you feel with direct eye contact?
- How much of a distraction would be: Corridor noise outside the room? Visible activity outside the room? Other people being able to look in?
- Would a very small room/very big room be off-putting for you?
- Do you feel comfortable about being alone in a room with me? (especially important in cross-gender relationships, or coaching/mentoring between an adult and a child)
- Do you prefer a lot of light, so you can make notes, or softer lighting, so you can think?

Best and worst environments

In this technique, the mentor or coach takes two sheets of paper (A3 is better than A4) and asks the learner to draw the worst possible environment for their meetings on one, and the best on the other. The more humour that can go into the exercise, the better. How might they avoid the characteristics of the negative picture and create as many as possible positive characteristics in the positive picture? Having established what is required, they can attempt to work out together where they might meet, how they would arrange the furniture and so on.

A critical view of building rapport as technique
Kate Hopkinson

Building rapport is the paradigmatic example of where *not* to use techniques. The essence of real rapport is 'authenticity'. This involves being present for – and open to – another person in a way that no technique (however skilfully wielded) will facilitate.

Authentic meeting between two people is the opposite of a pro-grammed series of moves, which are not engaged in for their own sake, but as a means to a pre-determined end. This is why 'Have a nice day' is counter-productive – the recipient knows only too well that this utterance has nothing whatever to do with a spontaneous expression of goodwill towards them as an individual and everything to do with selling burgers (or whatever). Consequently, being subjected to this type of formatted communication can be alienating, rather than bonding, in its effect.

Building rapport, if it is to be successful, has to be an un-studied, un-rehearsed response to *this* person, as the interaction unfolds.

But it is not just responsive – it is a reciprocal process, so the developing relationship co-evolves, in real time, in the space between participants.

What are the essential constituents of this reciprocity? For both, it is marked by carefully judged and authentic self-disclosure; coupled with evident attentiveness and sensitivity to 'who the other is', and 'where they are coming from'.

Often both self-disclosure and acknowledgement are largely tacit, concerned as much with what isn't being said, as what is.

So what *is* being said? What is the medium through which these tacit transactions can take place? The basic task of rapport building is to iden-tify and begin to explore an area of common ground, in order to test for common values, attitudes and experience.

The starting point for this is usually overtly trivial. It may be the weather, today's travel conditions, their team's latest result, whatever. The content is relatively unimportant, except in so far as it demonstrates sen-sitivity on the initiator's part to the recipient. Many women are familiar with the experience of being on the receiving end of supposedly rapport-building remarks by men, which were actually alienating because they involved incorrect and patronizing assumptions about the recipient (which may again reside more in non-verbal behaviour, than in what is said).

There is an apparently paradoxical exception to the above. This is where the coachee gives clear (though probably tacit) signals that they don't want to be there. If so, it may be more productive to move straight to a non-trivial confrontation:

Coachee (gives a series of monosyllabic answers to various overtures from the coach, accompanied by 'negative' non-verbal signals).

Coach: 'It sounds as if you'd sooner be anywhere than here. (Wryly) I'm starting to feel the same...'

Coachee (reluctantly): 'Yeah – I feel I've been pushed into this.'

Coach: 'How did that come about?'

Coachee begins to fill in the background – there is now something to explore together.

This exploration of common ground is the beginning of creating a joint problem-solving climate – where the coach and coachee are working alongside each other, both attempting to find a way of understanding the coachee's experience which will enable her or him to move forward, and develop.

Setting expectations

The sound of silence

It takes approximately 4.5 seconds of silence on the car radio for the average person in Western society to switch channels. Silence is a phenomenon we are ill-equipped to handle; we attempt to fill it as quickly as possible.

Yet silence truly can be golden. It is the quiet periods in a coaching or mentoring session where the deepest and most cathartic reflection occurs. Effective coach/mentors create golden moments by looking for and recognizing when silence is better than asking yet another question. Some coach/mentors begin a session with a short period of meditation, but our view is that this is usually only beneficial when:

- the learner hasn't decided what they want to talk about,
- the learner needs to establish some inner calm, in order to address an emotionally difficult issue.

The most important use of silence is to allow the learner to ruminate on the implications of a point that has just struck home. The ineffective or inexperienced coach/mentor may simply rush in with a follow-up question – pressing home the attack, as it were. The effective coach/mentor, on the other hand, allows the learner extra thinking time and allows the learner to decide when to move on. This can be very frustrating, particularly if the learner is an introvert and the coach/mentor an extrovert, but the reward of patience is almost always a deeper insight and/or deeper commitment to a new course of action by the learner.

The seven layers of dialogue

Dialogue in mentoring, and coaching can be regarded as having seven layers of increasing depth and impact. This broad technique provides some guidelines on how to develop the skills of dialogue at each level. It is useful to discuss expectations of both parties as to where they expect the relationship to start and where they would like to end up.

Social dialogue is about developing friendship and providing support/ encouragement.

How to develop social dialogue
- Demonstrate interest in the other person, in learning about them.
- Actively seek points of common interest.
- Accept the other person for who they are – virtues and faults, strengths and weaknesses.
- Be open in talking about your own interests and concerns.

Figure 1.2 **The seven layers of dialogue.**

Technical dialogue meets the learner's needs for learning about work processes, policies and systems.

How to develop technical dialogue
- Clarify the task and the learner's current level of knowledge.
- Be available when needed (just-in-time advice is always best).
- Be precise.
- Explain the how as well as the why.
- Check understanding.

Tactical dialogue helps the learner to work out practical ways of dealing with issues in their work or personal life (for example, managing time or dealing with a difficult colleague).

How to develop tactical dialogue
- Clarify the situation (what do and don't we know?).
- Clarify the desired and undesirable outcomes.
- Identify barriers and drivers/potential sources of help.
- Establish fall-back positions.
- Provide a sounding board.
- Be clear about the first and subsequent steps (develop a plan, with timeline and milestones).

Strategic dialogue takes the broader perspective, helping the learner to put problems, opportunities and ambitions into context (e.g. putting together a career development plan) and to envision what they want to achieve through the relationship and through their own endeavours.

How to develop strategic dialogue
The helper uses the same skills as for tactical dialogue plus the following:

- Clarify the broader context (e.g. who are the other players in this issue?).
- Assess strengths, weaknesses, opportunities and threats.
- Explore a variety of scenarios (what would happen if...?).
- Link decisions and plans closely to long-term goals and fundamental values.
- Consider radical alternatives that might change the game (e.g. could you achieve faster career growth by taking a sideways move into a completely different function?).

Dialogue for self-insight enables the learner to understand their own drives, ambitions, fears and thinking patterns.

How to develop dialogue for self-insight
- Ensure the learner is willing to be open and honest with himself/herself.
- The helper merely opens doors – it is the learner's journey of discovery.
- Give time and space for the learner to think through and come to terms with each item of self-knowledge.
- Be aware of and follow up vague statements or descriptions – help the learner be rigorous in their analysis.
- Explore the reasons behind statements – wherever possible, help the learner to establish the link between what they say/do and their underlying values/needs.
- Introduce tools for self-discovery – for example, self-diagnostics on learning styles, communication styles, emotional intelligence or personality type.
- Challenge constructively – 'Help me to understand how/why…'.
- Give feedback from your own impressions, where it will help the learner reflect on how they are seen by others.
- Helping the learner interpret and internalise feedback from other people (e.g. 360 appraisal).

Dialogue for behavioural change allows the learner to meld insight, strategy and tactics into a coherent programme of personal adaptation.

How to develop dialogue for behavioural change
All the skills above, plus the following:

- Help the mentee to envision outcomes – both intellectually and emotionally.
- Clarify and reinforce why the change is important to the learner and to other stakeholders.
- Establish how the learner will know they are making progress.
- Assess commitment to change (and if appropriate, be the person to whom the mentee makes the commitment).
- Encourage, support and express belief in their ability to achieve what they have committed to.

Integrative dialogue helps the mentee develop a clearer sense of who they are, what they contribute and how they fit in. It enables the mentee to gain a clearer sense of self and the world around them; to develop greater balance in his or her life, and to resolve inner conflict. It explores personal meaning and a holistic approach to living.

How to develop integrative dialogue

More than any other form of dialogue, this is usefully characterized as a dance, in which both partners take the lead in turns, often exchanging rapidly. It involves the following:

- Exploring multiple, often radically different perspectives.
- Shifting frequently from the big picture to the immediate issue and back again.
- Asking and answering both profound and naïve questions (often it is difficult to distinguish between them!).
- Encouraging the mentee to build a broader and more complex picture of himself or herself, through word, picture and analogy.
- Helping them write their story – past, present and future.
- Analysing issues together to identify common strands and connections.
- Identifying anomalies between values – what is important to the mentee and how the mentee behaves.
- Making choices about what to hang on to and what to let go.
- Helping the mentee develop an understanding of and make use of inner restlessness, and/or helping them become more content with who and what they are.

While these are not seven steps to helping heaven, they do represent increasing depth of reflection on the part of the mentee and a corresponding need for skills on the part of the mentor. A single mentoring session might delve into several layers. In general, establishing dialogue at the social level assists dialogue at the technical level; technical dialogue can evolve into strategic – and so on up the ladder.

The most effective mentors and coaches invest considerable time and effort in building their repertoire of skills, so they can both recognize the appropriate level of dialogue to apply at a particular point, and engage the mentee appropriately. Very often, the mentee has little or no experience of operating at the deeper levels of dialogue and the mentor has to work with them to establish successive layers of competence, one by one. In some cases – for example, alienated teenage criminals with little education and low self-esteem – even social dialogue is a struggle. It may take many sessions of building trust and practising dialogue, before the mentor can even begin to explore deeper issues with the mentee. This is one argument for extending the length of such relationships, so that there is time to build the mentee's skills of dialogue. It also suggests that providing additional help, through discussion groups, where mentees can learn the basic skills of dialogue in a more structured, formal manner, should be an element of mentoring programmes for such groups.

As structured mentoring matures as a helping discipline, it is important that the emphasis shifts from how we put people together to how we improve the quality and impact of the dialogue in which they engage. The concept of the seven layers has proven very helpful in directing attention to developing the necessary skills among professional mentors; it should also have considerable relevance for mentoring and coaching within organizations.

References

Clutterbuck, D. and Ragins, B. R. (2002). *Mentoring and Diversity*. Oxford: Butterworth-Heinemann.

Persaud, R. (2001). *Staying Sane: How to Make your Mind Work for You*. London: Bantam.

Chapter 2

Setting goals

Introduction

Knowing what you want, why you want it and how you are going to get it is one of the most difficult issues for people to tackle. Sometimes goals are just too big to get one's mind around, sometimes there are just too many options, sometimes we feel guilty about what we want, sometimes we experience conflict between our emotional and rational ambitions and at other times all of these may be true! Even when someone has clear goals and a path towards achieving them, they may lack the commitment to follow things through.

It is not surprising, therefore, that coaches and mentors often spend considerable time and effort in the early stages helping the learner work through these issues. Time spent on gaining clarity and commitment at this stage will be repaid many times over.

There is more to goal setting in coaching and mentoring than merely highlighting deficiencies and setting goals to fill the gap. Indeed, many authorities on coaching advocate not focusing in the first instance on deficiencies. For example Richard Boyatzis argues that it is better to specify an ideal self and then to work towards it (Boyatzis, *et al.*, 2004). An interesting recent book (Grayling, 2004) offers a rigorous philosophical exploration of what goodness, or the good life, is. This will help thoughtful coaches and mentors to construct a framework for helping others to consider these questions. Boyatzis and his collaborators suggest that we should develop learning plans (which are positive emotional attractors), rather than performance improvement plans (because these are negative emotional attractors). His behaviourally oriented research indicates that change is more likely to occur if people are working towards a positive ideal rather than trying to fill a negative deficiency, particularly at the start of the working relationship. Once progress is being made, then the gaps can be addressed.

The techniques in this chapter have been ordered from those that emphasize vision, capability and using strengths through to those that focus upon deficiencies, gaps and needs.

There are three predominantly visioning techniques – *Boyatzis, Visioning* and *The meaning of success*. Then there are some in-between techniques, *The cascade of change, The change balloon* and *Establishing the current reality*. We conclude the chapter with some gap or need techniques: *Extremes, Logic trees* and Joyce Russell's and Robert Smith's *Understand your habits* and *Is this the goal you really want?*

Techniques from vision to deficiencies

The Boyatzis technique

Boyatzis *et al.* (2004) suggest that, if you ask anyone about who has been the most helpful to them over their career and what they do, the results follow a pattern. Try this for yourself before reading on. Note down a maximum of 10 people who have been helpful in your career and list briefly what they did to develop you.

When we have done this we have found that the results confirm Boyatzis's supposition that 80 per cent of all the comments will be about extending dreams and reaching for new experiences. They are about clarifying and enlarging what it is to be successful and good.

Case study   **David's list**

David's list included the following:

- Challenging self-image.
- Develop a shared purpose.
- Build a group identity.
- Modelling becoming a good citizen.
- You can become more committed in your personal style.
- You can like yourself and thus be more likeable and helpful.
- Permission to focus on my own autonomy.
- Faith that I could do it.
- Excitement; challenge; possibility.
- You can fill this role for us.
- You can make this organization far more than it has been.
- We can professionalize and democratize the organization.

He reported that virtually all of these matched the Boyatzis prediction. People who highlighted his deficiencies didn't help him.

The next phase is to develop a new or clearer sense of your ideal self. With David the focus of coaching was upon deciding which parts of his sense of self he needed to let go of as well as which he needed to enhance. The experience was creative and liberating and enabled him to make some commitments that had hitherto blocked his development over an extended period. He reported that this was one of the most freeing experiences of development that he had ever been through.

Visioning

Visioning is a technique used in many coaching situations, but it is particularly powerful in goal setting. The core of effective visioning is the engagement of all the learner's senses – especially sight, smell, touch, and inner emotion. The developer invites the learner to close his or her eyes and imagine him/herself as they want to be in a specified period of time. The bigger and broader the goal, in general, the longer the forward projection will be. The question set may vary, but is likely in most cases to follow a progression along these lines:

Visualization
Where is it that you want to be (the place)?
Describe what you see around you – the environment, the people
How do you appear?
What are you doing? Why?
Describe how you feel. If you feel good, what is making you feel that way?
Describe how the people around you feel?
Describe what you hear?

Determination
How is this different from now?
How big is the gap in how you see yourself? How others see you?
How big is the gap in how you feel? How others feel?
How do you feel about that gap? Do you have a real desire to bridge it?

Actualization
What could you do to make the vision a reality?
What's your first step?

When and where to use visioning in goal setting
Visioning is best used when the learner is relatively relaxed. It requires the engagement/focus of the whole consciousness for someone to place themselves in a possible future. It can be used to explore and compare different goals – by analysing a set of different futures, the learner can begin to decide between them. For example, how does the scene appear

in two years' time, if you stay in the current company or department, compared with if you move on? How does the pain of divorce compare with the suffering of an unhappy marriage?

The approach can, however, be used in almost an planning/decision-making process where the outcomes will take some time to emerge.

Case study   Rosalyn

Rosalyn was a bright young professional in her mid-twenties, working for an international merchant banking house. She was also a talented singer, spending what free time she could take from a demanding, long-hours job practising or performing with amateur and, occasionally, professional bands. What she wanted emotionally was to become a singer full-time; intellectually, she knew she had a relatively secure, high-income job which she quite enjoyed.

She took her dilemma to an in-company coach when she had the option of a small but career-significant recording contract that would demand more time away from her job than she would normally be able to take. Could she perhaps get a sabbatical, or a reduced-hours contract, she asked.

Instead of focusing on the practicalities of her request, the coach used visioning to help her think through what she really wanted as a career. It rapidly became clear that what she really wanted was for someone to give her permission to follow her emotional instincts and become a full-time singer. Visioning two different futures showed that doing something she really enjoyed was as likely, if not more likely, to give her financial rewards. She quit, signed the contract, is now earning more than in her previous job and feels far more fulfilled. She has not yet completely fulfilled her vision of success, but she is less than 1 year into a 2-year projection. However, she is already using visioning to look further ahead, to receiving a Best Solo Singer of the Year award, presented by Robbie Williams!

The meaning of success

One of the most common forms of transference that occurs between coach/mentor and learners relates to perceptions of success. It is so easy for the coach/mentor to impose his or her assumptions about what success means upon the other party.

The generic definition of success we use is *achieving what you value*. Achievement on its own is not enough. It is quite common for people to make a fortune but be discontent. Achieving an outcome that is not important to you or is not something you particularly want is not success. Nor is achieving something someone else wants, unless what you value is pleasing that person. In short, people's perception of success varies widely and coach/mentors need to:

● recognize the validity of the other person's definition of success,
● refrain from imposing their own,
● help the learner clarify what success means to them,
● help the learner relate life and career goals to that meaning.

In this technique, the coach/mentor gives the learner a small number of generic success factors to consider. One set, which we use frequently is:

● money
● status or peer recognition
● job satisfaction
● work life balance.

The learner is then asked to allocate 10 points (no fractions allowed!) between these factors, according to how much they value each as part of what success means to them. Next they do the same calculation, but looking backward, say 10 years; then forward for the same amount of time. What changes do they see in success criteria between these dates?

It is not unusual for people to change their view of what makes for current success in the light of this discussion. It also helps the coach/mentor recognize where the learner is applying values different to his/her own, and to adjust their overall helping approach accordingly.

It can be useful to generate a longer list of success factors, treating the four listed above as a jumping-off point. On one occasion when one of us did this the mentee came up with:

● happiness
● doing good
● health
● family
● spirit
● making a difference
● autonomy/flexibility
● security.

Rather than use this longer list, it makes the activity centre upon the mentee's concerns if they generate their own list.

The cascade of change

The change cascade addresses the issue of commitment, from a stage model perspective. This recognizes that people go through a number of

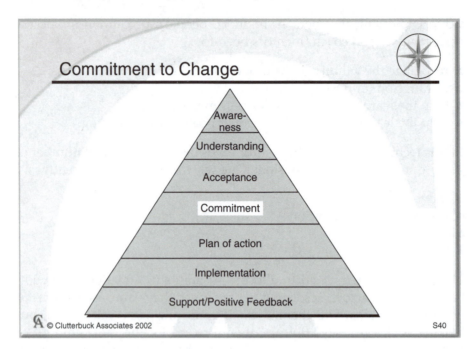

Figure 2.1   Commitment to change.

steps to achieve commitment, then several more to move from commitment to achievement, as in Figure 2.1.

Awareness of a requirement to change is unlikely of itself to stimulate action, unless the consequences of not doing so are immediate and dire. There may be intellectual understanding that it would be beneficial to be more skilled at a specific task or behaviour, but that is also true of hundreds of other tasks and behaviours – why should this one assume any sense of urgency or priority?

Understanding occurs when the need for change is brought into focus, usually by some external event, which underlines the benefits of taking action and the disadvantages of not doing so. Although the stimulus may be emotional, this is primarily an intellectual recognition and the sense of urgency can be rationalized away quite quickly. There may also be a clash of belief sets within the individual (for example, *I know I'm making myself ill eating chocolate, but I enjoy it*).

Acceptance occurs when the emotional and intellectual senses of urgency align. The benefits of action strongly outweigh those of inaction and the person is able to focus on this issue without too much competition from other issues that demand his or her attention.

Commitment puts the seal on acceptance. It involves a solemn promise, to oneself or to others, whose respect you value. It links achievement of the change goal with our sense of identity – our self-image. To fail is to diminish oneself. Commitment will not deliver results, however, without a *plan of action*. The plan will be of little use, if it is not implemented. And *implementation* requires *positive feedback*, both from oneself and from others, to reinforce the commitment. If, after initial effort, there is little sign of progress, it is common for enthusiasm to wane, and for old habits to reassert themselves as the effort-reward equation is re-evaluated.

The coach–mentor supports the learner through any of these stages, but will be most effective when the learner has at least reached the awareness stage.

Using the cascade is simply a matter of probing to see where the learner has reached in the various stages. If she or he is only at the awareness stage, it may be better in most cases to focus effort on issues, where they have achieved a higher level of commitment.

Case study   Jake

Jake is the owner-manager of a small IT services company. He prides himself on his drive and on how his business has survived two major downturns in the sector, in which many of his competitors went to the wall. When he married his long-time partner, he took his laptop on honeymoon with him. Jake has two children, but saw relatively little of them. One of his excuses was that they were 'too young to have a conversation with'.

Jake understood intellectually that he was not spending enough time with his family, but reasoned it would all be easier when the company was that bit bigger and he could hand things over to other managers. In reality, the bigger the company became, the more time he spent on work.

The crunch came when he was working at home one weekend. He was typing up an important and complex report and was so engrossed, he forgot to save what he was working on. Only when the screen went blank did he notice his 4-year-old son, holding the disconnected power cable. 'Time to play, daddy,' said the boy. For some reason he couldn't explain, instead of losing his temper, Jake found himself asking what had caused his son to do something so destructive.

When he rang his mentor on the Monday, Jake had two questions. 'How do I develop a plan to get my life back? And 'How do I make sure I stick to it?'

It was pretty obvious to the mentor where Jake was on the change cascade. The problem, as Jake himself had discerned, was how to keep him there and help him push himself into new behaviours until they became habitualized. The key in this case lay partly in the plan, which scheduled unbreakable family events into the diary every week – including collecting his son from nursery school on Fridays, which forced him to come home early,

(Continued)

and partly in the feedback process, wherein Jake and his family instituted a regular discussion over dinner, when they discussed what they had achieved together during the previous week and what they were going to do together the week coming. Both these ideas were generated by Jake himself, with guidance from the mentor.

In the 3 years since, Jake has relapsed twice, when work crises begin to take over. Each time, however, he has worked with his mentor to look again at his commitment and to find a way back. A new habit has now become ingrained. Whenever he has to neglect the family for a few weeks, they now take a short holiday to compensate and rebuild relationships.

The change balloon

Knowing exactly what you want and/or how important it is to you, are important elements in achieving commitment and getting started on the change journey. Among techniques useful in identifying priorities are *the change balloon*, which describes in a graphic way the process of choices that are involved in staying afloat.

In this process, the coach–mentor asks the learner to write down their wish list. The list may refer to a specific situation (for example, what they want in their next job, or the outcomes from an important negotiation) or to life in general. The coach–mentor draws a hot air balloon, with a large basket. Each wish will be written on a post-it, which becomes a weight, hanging on the side of the basket.

The coach–mentor now asks the learner to imagine that the balloon has sprung a slow leak. One of the weights will have to be cut loose. Which can they afford to drop? The item is deleted and recorded else-where as the lowest priority from the list.

One by one, the weights are allowed to fall until only one is left. How does the learner feel about the resulting priority rankings?

In discussing this process, mentees often say that they find it difficult to let go of any of the weights because they are all inter-related. It can be useful to note these links and to explore them later. If they want to work on one of the items, they will need to pay attention to those that are linked to it.

Case study   **Jane accompanies Angela on a balloon ride**

When Jane was working with Angela on this, they stuck the flip chart paper with the balloon on the wall. They then moved it up every time an item was taken out. When it was getting out of reach, Jane drew another hole in the balloon, and brought it down in reach again. This physical engagement was accompanied by laughter and also wails of concern from Angela about the difficulty of choosing between two attractive options. They avoided 'cheating' where two items were seen to cover each other, and kept them separate to force the hard choices – this is the work of this activity. They finished their discussion by considering the implications for Angela of what was left. Having the third party (the flip chart balloon and post-its) meant that Angela had relatively little to do in this discussion as Angela was so engaged.

Establishing the current reality

Most coaches are familiar with the GROW model. Establishing the learner's starting point is a critical step in the process and this is often done by getting them to rate themselves on a variety of factors, which may or may not be important to them. The coach may either come with a ready-made set of factors (see below for an example) or stimulate the learner to develop their own.

Some common areas for setting personal goals
- Being a better leader
- Managing my reputation
- Being a good parent
- Job satisfaction
- Meeting targets
- Being more in control (of work or life)
- Being more creative
- Having a clear conscience
- Developing my team
- Being happy
- Having a clear sense of direction
- Building my confidence.

The coach typically asks the learner to rank these factors in some way – for example, by placing them in baskets marked must do, should do, nice to do; or by locating them on an urgent/important matrix. The learner then selects the highest priority goals and defines more clearly what a particular goal actually means to them (i.e. achieves a greater level of precision about the desired state and how they would recognize it). The learner then rates him- or herself on a scale of 1 to 10 in terms of personal effectiveness.

The coach now asks the learner on each goal what a perfect score (10/10) would be like for them and negotiates for how much improvement they want to achieve within a given time frame.

Extremes

Extremes is a technique to help people put goals into context and decide whether or not (or how much) they really want to change. The authors have successfully used this technique to help each other resolve goal conflict.

As always in dealing with a problem or opportunity the developer starts by asking the learner to describe briefly the issue and the circumstances around it. She or he then helps the learner define a spectrum, on which the dilemma sits. Typically questions here are:

- What do you think you need to change from, to?
- How do you want circumstances to be different?

She or he then invites the learner to identify the extreme ends of this spectrum – for example, being completely honest with a customer and keeping them completely in the dark. The developer and learner then assign an emotive label to each of these extreme situations – in this case, for example, 'The Naked Truth' and 'Cover up'. Questions at this stage might be:

- Where are you on this spectrum now? (How have you dealt with it so far?)
- Where do you think you should be?
- Who says this is where you should be? Your inner self? Colleagues/your boss? The customer?
- What are the consequences of remaining where you are on the spectrum?
- What are the consequences of moving to the new position?
- Is there a position between which you would be more likely to commit to and to stick to?

When and where to use 'extremes' in goal setting

Extremes is best used when the learner is confused between what they feel obliged to do/ought to do and what they feel comfortable doing; or when the answer to a dilemma is unlikely to be clear-cut. It helps to sort out the level of their emotional commitment to the goal and, more often than not, to modify the goals into ones they are more likely to achieve.

Case study   **David**

Some time ago, one of the authors had been battered by a business partnership, from which he had withdrawn, feeling he had been badly cheated. He told himself that he had to learn to become less trusting and this view was reinforced by a host of other well-wishers around him. The problem was that he did not feel comfortable with making such a change, so he prevaricated and did nothing.

The peer mentoring relationship was the ideal place to explore this dilemma. The statement 'I need to become less trusting' was quickly translated into a spectrum, with 'trusting fool' at one end and 'suspicious bastard' at the other. Where was he now? About half-way between the median and trusting fool. Where was the pressure to be? About half-way between the median and suspicious bastard.

What were the benefits of being in the latter position? Less likelihood of being taken for a ride and more opportunity to oblige people to live up to their promises. What were the negatives? It would be counter to his natural instincts; it would alienate some clients and associates; and it would make relationships more transactional in nature.

What were the benefits of staying as he was? Trusting others resulted in a tremendous amount of loyalty; the gift of much free time as associates collaborated on development projects; and much more enjoyable relationships. The negatives? From time to time, someone will take advantage.

Looking at the balance of positives and negatives in each scenario, it soon became clear that there was a compromise solution, which involved relatively little behaviour change. Instead, it was possible to introduce more robust contracts, be more explicit about expectations of business partners and be more rigorous in taking meeting notes. Being cheated occasionally was a relatively small by-product, compared to the benefits of a more generous approach.

The relief he felt at not having to behave in ways that went against his personality and values was palpable.

Case study Rebecca

Rebecca had left her home town in Lancashire to go to university, after which she settled into a career in London. Her elder sister, Gemma, had married without taking further education, moved with her husband into a house near to her parents and concentrated on raising a family. Both sisters are in their late forties. Never close as children, they now have little in common and rarely see each other, except for family gatherings, such as when their father died last year. Their mother is now finding it difficult to cope on her own and the burden of looking after her falls largely on Gemma. The stress is clearly showing.

Gemma frequently calls, asking Rebecca to come up to help her. Rebecca has made the trip up once a month, on average, but finds it very difficult to fit this in with the demands of her job – especially the frequent overseas travel. It has gradually become obvious that Gemma resents Rebecca's comparative

(Continued)

wealth and lifestyle. Rebecca dreads the visits home, because of these emotional undercurrents. Her feelings of guilt were also affecting her work – she had become somewhat short-tempered and uncharacteristically forgetful.

The dilemma she brought to a mentor development workshop was: Should she confront her sister and bring the issues into the open, or simply slog on in the same way, knowing that it was only a matter of time before her mother dies?

Working with a workshop colleague, Rebecca established a set of extremes that seemed to sum up her dilemma. At one end was 'Go all out to build the friendship with Gemma'; at the other was 'Be a career-focused bitch'.

The pluses of building a friendship with her sister included removal of the stress and the knowledge that it would greatly please her mother, who still had enough of her marbles to sense the tension between her daughters. On the negative side, it would mean reducing her responsibilities and work and foregoing the promotion she had been working towards for a long time. She also admitted to herself that she didn't really *like* her sister and that the chances of success were small.

The pluses of focusing on her career were that she would not have the time conflict. She could simply send money. Her sister would be so offended that she would not talk to her – which was at least better than being constantly nagged at! On the minus side, she would lose the opportunity to spend time with her mother in her last days and she would feel guilty about destroying the last vestiges of family togetherness.

Where she was now, was struggling somewhere in the middle. Where she felt she ought to be was towards the 'build friendship' end. Where she wanted to be, she admitted to herself, was closer to the 'career-focused bitch' end.

Understanding these conflicting goals helped her rethink her position. She resolved to do a number of things. In particular, she would:

- sit down with her sister and explain what sacrifices she would have to make to visit her mother more frequently;
- offer to share the burden in other ways – by paying for a home help and gardener;
- Take her mother away on holiday with her, to give her sister a respite.

In this way, Rebecca found that she could stay as she was – steering a middle course – but do so more effectively and with less stress. Clarifying what could and could not be expected of her abated the sister's demands and she actually got closer to her mother, by spending holiday time with her, than she had ever done since she was a child. She still doesn't like her sister, but now accepts that as a fact of life!

Logic trees

People often don't start a developmental journey because they cannot see a clear path to their goal. The logic tree is a simple method of breaking down complex goals into more easily achieved steps.

Step 1: Ask the learner to define the goal as clearly as possible. Help them to refine this description to no more than ten words. Test the definition against SMART (specific, measurable, etc.).

Step 2: Explore what would need to be done to achieve the goal. For example, to become a team leader, a learner might need to demonstrate some key competences, to make their ambition known to particular people, to build confidence among peers in their ability and to acquire more knowledge about managing others.

Step 3: Break each element of step 2 into further sub-divisions and continue the same process, layer by layer, until each results in a series of actions that could be undertaken relatively easily and/or soon. For example, what could they do to demonstrate each of the key competences? How would they find or create opportunities to practise the skills involved? Where could they find appropriate coaching support?

Step 4: Begin to apply some timelines. When do they want to have achieved each of the lowest level objectives? Do they feel confident in their ability to do so? What timelines would be appropriate for the next level? Gradually work up through the process chart to the overall goal at the top.

Step 5: Step back and review the process. Does the goal now seem much more achievable than it did before? Have we missed any important elements? What milestones would it be appropriate to identify, where we should review progress and celebrate achievement so far?

Step 6: Regularly review with the learner where they think they have reached on the flow chart. Where progress falters, help them think through the issues and develop alternative strategies.

The example in Figure 2.2 illustrates in very simple terms a logic tree for becoming a confident public speaker. In using this technique for real, it helps to start with a fairly large sheet of paper (at least A3) and expect to use up most of the space.

Understand your habits
Joyce E A Russell, Robert H Smith School of Business, University of Maryland

This technique is based upon a framework of Canfield *et al.* (2000).

Successful people have successful habits. Unsuccessful people don't! Successful people don't drift to the top – it takes focused action, personal discipline, and lots of energy every day to make things happen.

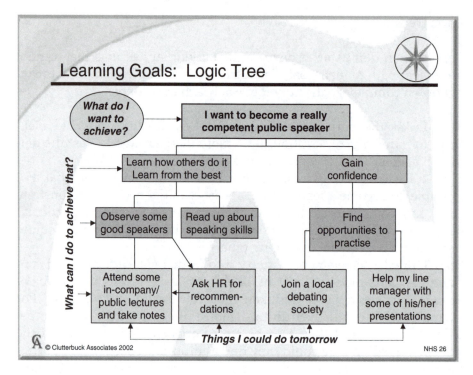

Figure 2.2   Logic tree example.

Understand your habits and be willing to change them to get the results you want. Up to 90 per cent of our normal behavior is based on habits! Add a *no exceptions* policy to your exercise plan, financial plan, family time, community activities. Your habits will determine your quality of life. The results of your bad habits usually don't show up until much later in life.

It may take you about 3–4 weeks to change a habit. At that point, it starts to become easier to engage in the new habit than to revert back to the old habit. Remember, if you keep on doing what you've always done, you'll keep on getting what you've always got.

Understand and change your habits
1. Identify habits that are holding you back.
   Example – I am not exercising enough
   Consequences – I don't feel I have enough energy, I can't lose weight
2. Identify a successful new habit.
   Example – I will exercise for 30 minutes three times a week
   Benefits – I will feel better, have more self-confidence
3. Develop a three-step action plan to jump-start your new habit.
   a) Get all walking equipment needed (shoes, clothes). Map out a trail where you live

    b) Develop a timeline for when you can exercise this coming week (times and days)

    c) Get support from others regarding your plan and times (e.g. if you need to get childcare assistance, etc.)

4. Identify your start date.
5. Share your individual plan with others and get their feedback and support.

Work on your priorities (the Power of Focus) – The 4-D Solution

Separate urgent tasks from your most important priorities. Focus on getting your urgent priorities dealt with. Use the 4-D Formula to help you prioritize:

    Dump it – learn to say 'no, I choose not to do this.' Be firm

    Delegate it – hand some tasks over to others

    Defer it – defer the issue to a later time and schedule a later time to do it

    Do it – do it now if it is an important project. Don't make excuses. Give yourself a reward for completing these projects.

Periodically ask yourself, 'Is what I am doing right now helping me achieve my goals?'

Establish your goals
1. Define your most important goals for yourself (don't use others' goals).
2. Make your goals meaningful (e.g. what are the rewards and benefits you envision?).
3. Your goals must be specific and measurable (e.g. how much more time do you want with your family?).
4. Your goals must be flexible (don't be so rigid that you lose good opportunities that come along).
5. Your goals must be challenging and exciting (e.g. what are the 100 things you want to do in your life?).
6. Your goals must be in alignment with your values (e.g. honesty, fairness, etc.).
7. Your goals must be well balanced (e.g. make sure you consider spending time with your family, leisure time, etc.). When you are 100 years old and people ask you 'If you had to live your life over again what would you do differently?', think about what you might say and plan your goals now to accomplish those things.
8. Your goals must be realistic – but remember, there are no such things are unrealistic goals, only unrealistic time frames!
9. Your goals must include contribution – you need to be a giver, not just a taker.
10. Your goals need to be supported.

It's Your Life ... Accept the Challenge!

'To laugh often and much; to win the respect of intelligent people and affection of children; to earn the appreciation of honest critics and endure the betrayal of false friends; to appreciate beauty, to find the best in others; to leave the world a bit better, whether by a healthy child, a garden patch or a redeemed social condition; to know even one life has breathed easier because you have lived. This is to have succeeded'.

Ralph Waldo Emerson

Is this a goal you really want?

We sometimes call it 'appraisal submission' – the situation when people agree to developmental goals imposed by others through the appraisal process, even though they have no heart for investing the necessary time and mental effort in them. Especially if you had had a relatively positive review, it seems churlish to object to suggestions for areas of potential improvement.

The reasons for such reluctance are many. For example:

- Not perceiving the issue to be serious enough (especially in relation to other changes, which you regard as having greater urgency).
- Having no emotional commitment.
- Inner conflict with one's values.
- A perception that the effort: reward ratio is inadequate.
- Self-confidence.
- 'I won't get the support I need'.
- A perception that the other party(ies) is not really that bothered whether the change happens or not – 'Next time, he/they will pick on something completely different'.

For the coach–mentor and the learner to invest resource and energy in pursuing a goal, to which the learner is not committed, is pointless. It is also likely to undermine the relationship.

References

Boyatzis, R., Howard, A., Kapisara, B. and Taylor, S. (2004). Target practice. *People Management*, 11 March, 26–32.

Canfield, J., Hansen, M. V. and Hewitt, L. (2000). *The Power of Focus*. Deerfield Beach, Fl: Health Communications.

Grayling, A. C. (2004). *What is Good?* London: Orion.

Chapter 3

Clarifying/ Understanding situations

Introduction

The techniques in this chapter are drawn from a wide range of disciplines, some well known, and others less so. What they have in common is that they help build contextual understanding.

Although the human brain has evolved to manage complexity, it has many limitations. Relatively few people can remember a string of eight or more numbers for more than a few seconds, for example; let alone repeat them in reverse order. Yet the complexity of living in the 21st century world is increasing rapidly and exceeds the relatively modest increase in average intelligence across developed country populations over the past 50 years.

Fortunately, there is a wide range of approaches available to help us to give structure to complex situations and thus simplify how we deal with them to the extent that we can handle the richness of the experience. However, a frequent issue for the coach/mentor working to help people in this way is to ensure that simplifying does not mean trivializing. Another issue is avoiding imposing one's own contextual understanding on the learner.

Dramatizing understanding

This section offers two techniques for enriching understanding by using metaphors, stories and drama. Some further uses of metaphor are explored in Chapter 4.

Effective metaphors and stories

The use of metaphor to help someone better understand or reframe a situation is a very old technique. An effective metaphor:

- establishes parallels between the situation as the individual sees it now and a different context;
- matches the listener's experience, particularly at an emotional level;
- uses strong imagery and language that captures the imagination;
- contains clear transitions or decision points, where choices have to be made;
- explores the impact of choices.

Case study **Claude**

An example of good use of metaphor concerns Claude, who was head of training and development for the continental European operations of a multinational services company. Having built an integrated team and delivered on some challenging targets, he was asked to take over the less able team in the UK and merge the two groups into one. A powerful metaphor was the battleground. Where were the battle lines drawn? Which troops were regulars and which were mercenaries, liable to change sides depending on how the merger was handled? What were the pressures to create distrust and conflict; and those that could be used to avoid a battle altogether? If he did not spill some blood, would an uneasy, potentially rebellious peace be worse than an initial conflict that settled matters? The analysis provided a range of alternative tactics, from which he was able to select.

Although many adults see telling stories to be a childish pursuit, it is in fact a core skill for the effective coach/mentor. The parables of Jesus are still among the most powerful examples of teaching through story. Story telling is also a skill that is hard to do well. Regaling the learner with your old war stories and personal anecdotes is not recommended – indeed, as coaches and mentors we require the ability to hold back on our own stories, until we are sure that they form an appropriate metaphor for the learner. Equally, deciding between using a real story, from our own experience, or one taken from the wider world of myth and reality, requires good situational judgement.

A three step model for using metaphor to effect change

A model buried in our files provides a useful and simple process for helping a learner focus on a behavioural change and its meaning for them.

Step 1 is to select the metaphor. Several alternatives may be discussed before the learner identifies one that they feel has sufficient relevance to their own situation. Place the learner within the metaphor: examine their role and fill in as much of the context and background as possible, labelling other players if appropriate.

Step 2 embeds the metaphor in reality. The coach/mentor asks for examples of where and how the metaphor has been played out in real life. If some elements of these examples do not fit the metaphor, they are recorded and set aside for subsequent discussion. Next the discussion moves to how the metaphor has evolved in the past and how it might be expected to evolve in the future. Exploring the metaphor from the viewpoint of other players also enriches the understanding of the issues.

Step 3 asks the learner to extract lessons from the metaphor. How does it make them feel? (Optimistic or pessimistic? Challenged or bored?) What aspects of the metaphor have the greatest impact on their work and/or life? What elements of the metaphor would they like to change?

In some cases, progress for the learner may mean recognizing that this metaphor will always bring them less success or less satisfaction than they want and that they need to develop a different metaphor, one that describes more closely what they want. The coach/mentor can then work through the cycle with them again, until they have a clearer perception of the new metaphor and the role they aim to play within it.

All the world's a play

Metaphor is a powerful method of provoking both intellectual and emotional exploration of the dimensions of a situation. It enables learners to use their creative imagination to connect with aspects of the situation that they might otherwise neglect.

One of the reasons issues often seem complex and difficult to resolve is that the individual is a participant at several levels. To understand human interaction beyond the superficial level, for example, we have to observe what is happening within us, extrapolate what is happening within other people involved, and step back and look at the interaction, as if we were someone disconnected from the interaction. It's rather like watching a Pirandello play, where the audience also becomes the actors and vice versa.

Using the metaphor of the play, the coach/mentor helps the learner take the perspective of each of the principal actors, including him- or herself. Then the learner is asked to take the perspective of the audience and finally, that of the playwright. The latter is often the most difficult, but also the most rewarding, because it raises the question of who is writing the script. If nobody, then there is a role waiting to be filled, with the learner being one candidate to do so.

The metaphor of the play can be used in a variety of ways, with the learner having options to change the characters, the roles, the script or even the audience. Each alteration provides an opportunity to open up new and different options.

Contextual mapping processes

This section contains Steve O'Shaughnessy and Sharon Collins's *Role environment mapping*, which is a context-enlarging technique, and Dianne Hawken's *An holistic/ecological/person-in-environment approach in mentoring*, which uses a comprehensive checklist to enrich appreciation of context.

Role environment mapping
Steve O'Shaughnessy and *Sharon Collins, The Quo Group Ltd*

The focus of this technique is helping people identify issues they may not be aware of.

Coaching or mentoring can start from a set of needs and issues identified by the learner or their boss with an expectation that they will be addressed. These 'presented' needs are often merely the tip of an iceberg where more critical issues are under the surface outside the initial awareness of the individual. A process that helps progress from the known (presented) to the unknown (outside awareness) is REM (Role Environment Mapping).

In early interactions with a coach or mentor, presented issues are frequently those believed to impact on working performance, satisfaction or career progress. Issues may be couched in very global terms (e.g. 'I feel overwhelmed by the amount I have to do and the number of people I have to deal with') or quite narrowly specific (e.g. 'If I could perform better at meetings and presentations I would be more successful').

We believe that REM is useful in addressing these early, 'presented' issues and is particularly relevant in the following coaching/mentoring situations:

- the development challenges of 'high potential'/'high talent' people;
- people facing step changes in their role responsibilities or scope;
- those who find their role impacted by significant organizational or similar context changes.

REM draws on a number of theories and approaches relating to awareness building and personal change including:

- Mind Mapping – a well known process to free up new ideas and connections between the familiar and more creative alternatives.

- Applied Behavioural Analysis – which enables an understanding of the impact of antecedents or consequences on learnt patterns of behaviour.
- Gestalt Theory and other models of personal growth and change – which illustrate how personal change can be blocked at important stages in the cycle of experience (e.g. a need can be 'deflected' away from awareness towards a familiar behaviour pattern that blocks development).

While REM draws on these theoretical insights, it is applied very pragmatically and can help deliver business and personal development goals.

How does REM work?

REM is driven by a philosophy that sees coaching as a vehicle for individual transformational change. The coach or mentor uses probing questions to facilitate and extend the learner's awareness of the present situation and the blocks and barriers to change at the organizational, interpersonal and intrapersonal levels.

REM can operate at several levels according to the starting awareness of the individual and the issues they need to tackle. For a newly promoted executive-level manager who has moved from a functional role to one which has much wider responsibilities, the map would be built up by focusing on questions such as:

- What is the range of objectives that must be delivered?
- Which of these are critical in the short term?
- Which have hidden, implicit or changing parameters?
- Who are the key people to be influenced?
- Who are the allies, rivals, potential threats?
- What changes can you anticipate?
- Who can you trust to deliver?
- What things get in the way of success?
- Who/What do you get frustrated with?
- What deflects you from your task?

Using questions like these, a map is built up of the individual in a role, and in context. During the questioning and mapping process learning points and blockages begin to surface.

The map includes defining forces which the individual exerts (or fails to exert) upon their environment and those pressures with which they have to contend. Clarifications of these include getting reality into their perceptions of delivery requirements, organizational politics, hidden and explicit change agendas and their own self-limiting beliefs and barriers to change.

Application and limitations

This approach is appealing at first sight because it is disarmingly simple. It enables particular issues to be picked up or mapped further at a deeper level. Here the skills and capabilities of the coach are critical in determining how far to take the process. Quite deep tensions can be uncovered so sensitivity is essential. High level coaching often requires entering some uncomfortable and unexpected territory for the coachee in a way that feels relatively safe or positive for him or her. At this point, the effectiveness of the coach in relation to trust, intimacy and empathy is vital as is an understanding of when to draw back from exposing an issue which may be unhelpful or too raw for the individual. REM is also not recommended where the learner is averse to 'psychologically' or 'behaviourally' oriented thinking or where they have become used to operating without this level of awareness and for whom it may be potentially disabling to re-orientate their sense of self in relation to role expectations.

An holistic/ecological/person-in-environment approach in mentoring
Dianne Hawken

This approach to mentoring reflects the value in recognizing the whole – as John Donne (1571–1631) said: 'No man is an island, entire of itself'.

At the start of a mentoring relationship we tend to focus on the mentee and their particular issues in the workplace. When we are working with inexperienced people or someone new to a position this is entirely appropriate. But when mentoring senior people we are providing a space for in-depth reflection, the exploration of broader issues and the discovery of other perspectives. Alternative viewpoints and other contributing influences are all part of the macro-environment within which we work. It is useful to identify those factors, especially those beyond our control. We can give our attention to what is within our power to change and develop an action plan, and then consider how we will respond to that which is beyond our influence.

This approach has its origins in systems theory in the social work arena. Systems theory encourages social workers to look beyond clients as isolated, independent units and look at the wider social systems. The ecological systems approach is concerned with the person's ability to negotiate, accommodate, adapt and survive in their environment and the dynamic interaction between people and their environment.

By considering the many and diverse systems that make up the whole environment we can expand the horizons of opportunity and understanding. Seeing the impact each system has on another, and the ripple effect, highlights the interdependence of everything. People often see where they can 'make a difference' and where to put their energies (and where not to). The ecological approach fits well for those cultures, like the Maori in New Zealand, who do not compartmentalize people and the environment, who value co-operation, family and community, the 'we' not the 'I', the connection to the land, sky and water and the significance of things spiritual.

For more linear thinkers this way of reflecting may initially appear cumbersome but in time the benefits of examining all the pertinent systems and their interactions clarifies, deepens understanding and illuminates future action.

The systems
1. The Mentee's work
2. The Mentee
3. The Mentor
4. The Mentoring Relationship
5. The Team
6. The Organization
7. The Work Environment
8. The Wider Context – social, economic, environmental.

Some questions for the mentor to ask/consider
1. *The mentee's work*
   Tell me about your work. What do you do? How? Where?
   What is particularly satisfying? Why is that?
   What part of your work is stressful/challenging? What makes it like that?
   What would you like to reflect on?
   What did you do? What happened then? What were the consequences?
   How did you feel about that? What did you want to happen?
   How would you have liked it to happen?
   How could that have been achieved? What would you have done differently?
   What resources would be useful in dealing with these kinds of situation again?
   What other options are there? Who are your allies? Who can you involve?
   What might happen if you did … ? How would you handle that?
   What might be a metaphor for this?
   How would you describe the interaction?
   If someone else were telling this how would they describe it, what would they say to you? What would they do?
   What supports do you have for your work? What do you need? How can you access the support you need?

What skills do you have? What are you good at? What needs development? How can you acquire these skills and knowledge?

2. *The mentee*

What is going on for you now? What is happening to you physically? Why do you think this is so?

Have you responded like this before? How do you usually respond? Have you come across this before?

What do you notice about the way you work? What patterns do you see? Why do you think these situations recur for you? Do you want to change anything? How might you begin? And then?

How do you see yourself in this role? How similar or different is it from other roles you have been in?

What do you want to say that you are not saying?

What makes it difficult for you? Why? What would make it easier for you?

What do you do to keep stress at bay? How are you balancing work and life outside of work? What impact is this having on life beyond work?

What are your personal goals? How do you want your life to unfold?

3. *The mentor – Questions to reflect on silently*

What am I experiencing/feeling? Is that what the mentee may be experiencing?

What image comes to mind?

Who does the mentee remind me of?

What past experiences of mine are being triggered? Do I need to explore this issue of mine with *my* mentor? Is this a distraction or may it help the mentee?

Is this my agenda or the mentee's?

Plus the same questions as the Mentee in 2 above.

4. *The mentoring relationship – Questions to reflect on silently*

What is going on between us? Is there a power issue?

Is it mentee-led and focused?

What are the accountabilities? Is there a developing conflict of interest?

Are there any blocks/barriers that are hindering the development of this relationship?

How can deeper trust develop?

Is there a parallel process going on?

When will be the time to dissolve the relationship?

5. *The team*

Where do you fit into the team? What part does the team play in this?

What are the team dynamics? What power issues are there?

How does the team fit in to the rest of the organization? How would the team see this?

What impact could this have on the team?

How could you engage your colleagues? What resources can the team supply?

What needs to change? How can you influence change?

6. *The organization*

Describe the organizational structure. Is it congruent with the goals and core business?

How does this affect the work environment?

Who can you discuss this with in the organization?

What systems are set up to respond to this? What needs to be considered?

Do they fit for this situation? What needs to be developed or challenged?

What resources can you access? Who do you need to liaise with?

What obstacles do you have to overcome? How will you do that?

What is the organizational culture? What effect does this have on you and your work?

How do you think the Board see this issue? What advice would they give you? How can you convey to them your perspective? What would convince them?

7. *The work environment*

What part does Information Technology have to play now and in the future?

What Code of Ethics/Standard of Practice underpins the work? What ethical tensions are there?

Who are your stakeholders? What are issues for each group? What is most crucial now?

Who are your clients and customers? What networking opportunities are available?

What strategic alliances can you make?

Who are your competitors? What gives you the upper hand? What added value do you give?

What are the current industry issues being grappled with?

Where is your business positioned? Where do you want it to be?

What is the funding/financial situation currently?

8. *The wider context*

Social

What part does gender/sexual orientation play here?

What cultural values come into play and take priority?

What values are taking priority here?

What spiritual beliefs may be important?

What is the predominant/minority view on family commitments?

How is this influencing the decisions?

Is this discriminatory? How might it be seen? By different groups?

To what extent is this situation influenced by language difficulties?

How do you respond to the issues that multiculturalism raises?
How can you use the media for a positive outcome?
Economic
What government policies are influencing this direction? What are the expectations of funders? Contract requirements? How does this policy impact? What can you or others in the organization do about it?
What laws impact? Are changes pending?
What do you see are the global forces that will impact on you in the near future? What can you control/not control?
Where will technology take this in the future?
Environmental
What effect will this have on the environment?
What responsibility do you have towards preserving the environment? How far does this go? Who has the say?

Circles of empowerment

This simple approach, which has much in common with the Circles of Disclosure technique in Chapter 1, is used to help the learner to establish those personal attributes that are sources of real or potential advantage, and those that are sources of disadvantage. Of course, many attributes have both positive and negative perspectives.

The learner is asked to identify as many aspects of their personality and background as possible, and to locate them vis à vis a line that represents the border between being a positive or negative factor in the specific context under examination. The context might perhaps be career progression in a particular organization or profession, being able to influence an important decision, or being able to achieve a specific level of performance in a sport. Circles entirely below the line indicate a severe hindering factor; those entirely above the line are enabling of the contextual goal. Those straddling the line have both positive and negative elements.

Having identified each of these elements, the coach/mentor helps the learner define what they can do to:

• make more of the positives;
• reduce the impact of the negatives;
• manage the line-straddling issues more effectively.

An optional intermediate stage (and one that differentiates this approach from SWOT analysis) is to discuss how large each circle should be. The bigger the diameter, the greater its impact on the goal and the higher the priority it should acquire in the dialogue between coach/mentor and learner.

Case study   **The MBA**

Circles of empowerment often prove useful in helping a learner from an eth-nic or gender minority understand the scope and sources of disadvantage they face in an organization. In the example below, the enabling factors include having a degree, being articulate and being ambitious. Hindering fac-tors are having the 'wrong' accent (i.e. not one associated with being edu-cated), lacking access to networks that provide access to senior managers, family commitments and not having enough track record of working on high profile projects. Line straddling factors are being black and being female (in this organization, positive action policies have been instituted).

   The learner, whose situation this example describes, chose to focus on two factors to increase the balance of advantage over disadvantage. She signed on, with some financial help from the company, for an MBA; and she used the mentor to introduce her to a range of senior managers, who she cultivated purposefully.

Identifying components of an issue

Stepping out/stepping in

Observation of effective mentors at work indicates that they have the tal-ent of keeping dialogue moving, primarily through switching perspec-tive. They rarely allow the learner to remain in the same mental state for long. They constantly shift the nature and style of the questions they ask. Analysis of how they change perspective suggests that they move around the quadrants of the matrix in Figure 3.1.

   Stepping into the box is about acknowledging the individual's own perspectives, joining them to try to understand what they are thinking and feeling, and why. Some people may come at an issue from a purely rational viewpoint, not wanting to explore their emotions for fear of what they might discover about themselves. Others may simply be too caught up in the emotion of a situation to think about it rationally.

   Stepping out of the box is about helping them to distance themselves from the issue, either to examine it intellectually from other people's or broader perspectives; or to help them empathize with and understand the feelings of other protagonists in the situation under discussion.

   To truly understand and deal with an issue, it is frequently necessary to explore it from each of these perspectives. A small insight into one perspective can generate progress in another and a skilled coach/mentor uses frequent shifts of questioning perspective to generate these incre-mental advances.

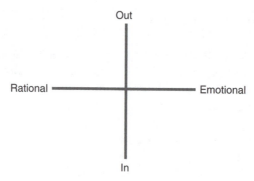

Figure 3.1   Stepping in/stepping out.

Case study   Jill

Jill came to her mentor in tears. She had just been bawled out publicly by her boss, in front of colleagues at a meeting. Her first question to her mentor was: *Should I resign?* Rather than address this issue, the mentor began to question her about her feelings. *What did she feel when the incident happened? How did she feel about it now? Might her feelings change after she had slept on the matter?*

The mentor then switched from the emotional, in the box quadrant to the rational, in the box quadrant. *What actual harm has this done to your self-esteem? Your ability to do the job? Your career prospects? Is this a one-off incident, or has it happened before?*

She next moved to rational, outside the box. *Would Jill's colleagues really be likely to use this incident against her? Were there wider issues of team morale here? Of team performance?*

Moving on to emotional, outside the box, the mentor asked: *What do you think your boss was feeling that made him do something so uncharacteristic? How do you think he feels about it now?*

The mentor then made shorter visits to each of the boxes as follows:

Do you enjoy your job normally? (emotional, in the box)
Are you good at it? (intellectual, in the box)
How do you want the relationship between you and your boss to be? (emotional, out of the box)
Do you think you have a responsibility to your colleagues, yourself and your manager to confront and deal with this issue constructively? (intellectual, out of the box)
How could you make it easier for your manager to accept and discuss the impact of his behaviour? (intellectual, out of the box)

Do you have the courage and commitment to talk to him now? (emotional, in
   the box)
Would you like to rehearse how you are going to open the discussion? (intellectual,
   in the box).

Jill asked her manager for a meeting as soon as possible that day. She
turned up feeling very nervous, but had only gone a short way into her
rehearsed discussion, when the manager stopped her, apologized and then
spent half an hour telling her about the pressures that had made him behave
as he did. Not only was he being driven hard by his boss, but he was des-
perately worried about his wife, who had just been diagnosed with breast
cancer. Unconsciously at the time, Jill found herself using the same questioning technique with him, to work out how she and the rest of the team could
support him through this stressful period. He was adamant that he did not
want his domestic problems more widely known, but agreed with Jill a working plan that distributed many of his responsibilities among the team, to free
him up to concentrate on the other issues. Having started a few hours
before, doubting her ability to stay with the firm, Jill emerged from the meeting with a much higher feeling of her own standing. Some months later, in an
emotional speech at a team away-day, her manager publicly recognized the
support she had given.

Unravelling the past to open up options for the future

It has been said that coaches and mentors do for your future what a
shrink does for your past. The techniques in this section seek to join the
past, through the present, to the future.

Career pathing

It's frightening sometimes how often people keep repeating the same
mistakes, particularly in terms of career choices. Career pathing is a simple approach to helping people learn lessons from previous career decisions, which they can apply to future decisions.

On a large sheet of paper, the coach encourages the client to write
down an early career choice – for example, which degree course to
take at university. How many other options did they have at this
time? Why did they choose this particular one? What advice, if any, was
available to them? How did they internalize that advice? How do they
feel about the choice? (Given the opportunity, would they choose differently now?)

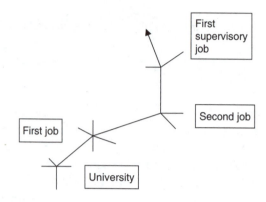

Figure 3.2   Career pathing.

The coach takes the client through a series of decision points, producing a map that looks something like the figure above.

In many cases, it might not have been a matter of making choices so much as drifting into a set of circumstances, where the choice was made for the client. Some choices may have expanded the range of future options, others severely constrained them. The coach helps the client analyse each of the pivotal points in his or her career, drawing out lessons concerning the nature and management of the process. Projecting this into the future involves questions such as:

- What pivotal decision points are likely to come in the next 24 months or so?
- To what extent have you prepared for these?
- Who will you want to consult and when?
- Will these expand or reduce your range of options?
- What values will you want to apply to the decision?
- How are you going to make sure you exert control over this next step in your career direction?

Case study   **Martin takes charge of his career**

Martin is a senior manger in a public sector organization. The organization was undergoing rapid and drastic change as the politic masters reshaped both its structure and scope. He felt frustrated that his ambitions of becoming a chief executive seemed to be receding, rather than getting closer. 'It's the sense of feeling impotent that really get to me', he told his mentor.

Using the career pathing exercise, Martin very quickly realized that virtually all the career moves he had made had been decided for him, or had been inevitable consequences of doing a reasonable job in the post before. While that had been successful in a relatively stable environment, it didn't seem such a sensible tactic in an unstable one. Moreover, when he benchmarked his career against that of more successful contemporaries, he realized that the main difference was that they *made* many of the opportunities that came their way.

He and the coach therefore worked together to develop a plan to open up more options for his next career move, against a background of several different scenarios for the organization. Important aspects of the plan included developing a much wider set of networks, both inside and outside the public sector, and taking on a number of projects, which would increase his general marketability.

Retro-engineered learning

The newcomer to a team is often at a severe disadvantage. Many of the tacit rules and assumptions, by which the team operates, are unconscious and far from obvious. Although some organizations make it easier by encouraging newcomers to question and challenge accepted practice ('Why on earth do we do it like that?!'), the reality in many cases is that newcomers are expected to learn the ropes rather than undo the rigging. Being too confrontational about the way things are done can be seen as threatening by established colleagues and as questioning their competence.

Retro-engineered learning is a relatively unthreatening way of giving the newcomer access to the evolution of culture and working practice. The case study given below illustrates the process.

Case study   Norman and Bernardo learn from the past

Norman is the head of operations at an international charity, which has projects all over the developing world. It is a demanding job, for both him and his team and sometimes harrowing. Tough decisions often have to be taken – for example, whether to leave staff in an area of high civil unrest and risk their lives or withdraw them, knowing that clients will suffer and perhaps die as a result. He had recently appointed a new regional head for Latin American operations, but the appointment didn't seem to be working out.

When he discussed the problem with his coach, it emerged that this wasn't the first recruiting problem he had experienced. Of his team of six, three had been appointed in the shoes of a failed predecessor. 'It's a tough job and people don't always work out', he explained. 'But I have to ask myself if I'm part of the problem. And I don't know'.

The main problem with the new Latin American manager, it seemed, was his inability to accept that long-proven routines were essential. He had come from another international-aid organization and before that from the private

(continued)

sector and had a strong instinct for approaches that solved the problem first then sorted out the bureaucracy. This caused conflict with both Norman and some of the new manager's peers. Norman was coming under pressure from his own boss to 'sort this guy out'.

The coach suggested using retro-engineered learning to ensure that the new regional manager understood why things were done in the way they were. A meeting was arranged between the three of them, where the coach acted as facilitator. The discussion went something like this.

Norman, when you were given the job of setting up the regional structure, what were your starting points?

Bernardo, having heard that, what would you have done to set up an efficient operation?

What did you actually do, Norman? (Norman explained the constraints he was operating under and the factors that shaped the decision-making processes.)

With what you know now, Bernardo, what would you have done differently? (Bernardo thinks deeply and outlines a broad strategy.)

Was that an option for you, Norman? What did you actually do? What constraints were you operating under?

Accepting the strategy that Norman had to work with, Bernardo, what would you have done to create an efficient reporting system?

And so on, until the present.

Throughout this discussion, the coach ensured that neither Norman nor Bernardo were judgemental about decisions and practices. The past was done, he explained. While we were not able to change it, and there may be decisions we regretted, by understanding the past we could be more realistic about current decisions. To Bernardo, the history of the operations function was mostly new information. The more he understood about the way the structure and systems in which his job operated had evolved, the more empathetic he could be to his colleagues' concerns. For Norman, reviewing the decision-making processes in hindsight provided a number of lessons that could be applied to current dilemmas.

The process of learning together forged a bond between Norman and Bernardo, which continued to grow. Because he could now put his criticism of the system into context, Bernardo was able to make much more acceptable arguments for re-assessing some key aspects of the operations and Norman authorized him to work with two of his colleagues to develop new approaches.

Reference

Buzan, T. (1995). *Use Your Head*. London: BBC Books.

Chapter 4

Building self-knowledge

Introduction

In many cultures self-knowledge is the fount of wisdom. In Sanskrit there is a term *rasa*, which means 'the delight of tasting one's own consciousness' (Anderson, 1996, p. 8). The precept on the gate of the oracle at Delphi was 'Know thyself'. Bagwan Shree Rajneesh said in a book *Neither This nor That*, which has been long out of print, that a much divorced film star might wonder why the women he marries all turn out to be bitches. Or, Bagwan wonders, why do we think we will be happy in a palace when we are not happy in our hovel. He suggests that it is useful to consider that wives and palaces do not exist except in our own imagination. Again, as the poet John Milton said in the ferment of the Protestant revolution, 'All are called to self-instruction, not only the wise or learned'.

So, one of the functions of mentoring and coaching is to enhance awareness of the degree to which we make our own lives. Much of this work seems to be directed at accepting the part that we have played in creating our own world. With both highly advantaged senior executives and with mightily oppressed disadvantaged groups, we notice a similar syndrome – the temptation to ascribe such good fortune as we have to ourselves and the corresponding desire to blame everything that goes wrong on others. This chapter sets out approaches that we have found useful in addressing these perceptions.

There are four sections:

- Opening up the learner's values.
- Changing belief sets.
- Bringing stereotypes into the open.
- Understanding one's life and career.

Opening up the learner's values

Mari Watson offers a focused way of *eliciting values*, based on the principle of taking a small incident, rather than discussing every aspect of the learner's life. The second technique, *taboo areas*, uses a questionnaire to get into difficult areas.

Eliciting values
Mari Watson

Sometimes clients (and coaches) find it a difficult or lengthy process to elicit the client's values in a consistently structured effective way.

Knowing the client's values helps them to make fulfilling choices, take appropriate decisions, formulate action plans, set goals, and lead a balanced life. It raises the client's self-awareness of how their feelings and behaviour are affected by actions and events that support or challenge their values.

The client is asked to identify special, peak moments in their lives which were particularly rewarding or poignant. The technique is based on one of a series of value clarification exercises in Whitworth *et al.*, (1998). It is most effective when the client selects a specific 'moment' – or there will be too much 'experience' to allow pinpointing of specific values. When the client has a specific moment in mind ask:

- What was happening?
- Who was there?
- What was going on?
- What was important about that?
- What else?

Listen carefully to the words the client uses and how their voice changes. Periodically pause and test the words used to see which values the client responds to. For example, this was drawn from a client interview:

> An important time in my life was when I was changing career. I was on the brink of making a big change, and saw the horizon stretched out in front of me. I was more than a little nervous, but the sense of possibilities was immense. I was spending a lot of time with my family, talking about the future. Their support was vital to nurture my dream and allow it to grow. They were honest with me – I value that honesty thing. I was being told that what I was doing was right for me. I knew that, but I needed to be told to be 100 per cent certain. I was starting to re-train too, and I love

learning and gaining knowledge. Also I like to 'be alone', and studying gave me that. And most of all it just felt right. I didn't feel uncomfortable.

This description gives a clear indication of the client's values:

- Limitless possibilities
- The community of family
- Security and safety
- Acknowledgement
- Truthfulness
- Knowledge
- Space alone.

Once a list has been established, ask the client to expand on each one by using questions such as:

- What does truthfulness mean to you?
- Can you make it specific – is it truthfulness or integrity or truth?

This exercise can be repeated and reviewed to ensure that as the client's self-awareness grows, their understanding of their values becomes deeper and more effective for them.

The list of values can also be used to inform decision-making using a values-based decision matrix, where the client lists their values and scores them out of 10 on their level of satisfaction. They can be challenged to take decisions based on how their values are respected or ignored for each outcome.

This can also be used to review life-balance issues for clients using the scores as stimuli for action.

There are other ways of eliciting values based on this model which may appeal to different clients and coaches, such as asking the client:

- to list the *must have* in their life;
- to take what is important to them, and what others say about them, to an extreme – and focusing on what the value might be;
- to describe a time in their lives when they felt angry, frustrated or upset, and reversing the descriptions of what shows up.

Defining what a value is need not be contentious – it is after all, most important that this exercise means something powerful to the client, and gives the coach a series of insights into what is important. To make this exercise most effective, ask the client to describe what values mean to them at the very start. It may help to work from a list of examples to prompt yourself and the client when words fail.

Sample list of values

Humour, fun, honesty, directness, partnership, family, reward, service, contribution, excellence, independence, autonomy, freedom, security, love, acknowledgement, limitless possibilities, success, adventure, danger, recognition, performance, community, friendship, power, strength, freedom of choice, empowerment, belief, trust, energy, joy, nurturing, creativity, integrity, lightness, discovery, feeling, winning, teaching, learning, sensitivity, relationships, space, peace.

Taboo areas

There are some topics that many people find difficulty in talking about. As a general principle, the more areas that mentors are comfortable in discussing, the more likely we will be to be able to respond to the concerns of our mentees.

This technique can be used to consider the possible taboo areas listed and rate how difficult you or your coachee would find it to talk about each. 0 = No difficulty; 1 = Slight difficulty; 2 = Moderate difficulty; 3 = Strong difficulty; 4 = No way. There are some blank spaces to list some other areas that have this taboo quality for you.

Choose two or three areas that have a degree of difficulty that makes them a bit of a challenge to discuss. Grayling (2004), in his analysis of the good life, summarizes Epicurus's view that there are four areas which we find difficult and that we need to address: god, death, pleasure and suffering. These areas are often taboo in organizations so this short list may be used rather than the long list in Figure 4.1.

Explore examples in this area. This can be an occasion when you or your coachee have displayed a quality or dealt with a difficult area well, or, more of a challenge, where there has been a failure to deal with the quality or area satisfactorily.

Changing belief sets

Belief sets are pervasive, hard to notice and harder to shift. A talented executive coach, Paul O'Donovan Rossa, was coaching a senior manager in a multinational who was struggling to be in the here-and-now. Paul noticed that his watch was not showing the right time, and it turned out that it was kept permanently five minutes fast, so he would never be late. Paul thought that a first step in being here-and-now would be to live in the same time as everyone else. His coachee found it a grounding experience.

We have two examples in this section from other contributors. Sandra Henson's *Challenging deeply held beliefs and assumptions* is a

Taboo Area	Rating 0–4	Example
Golf		
Emotions at work		
Failure		
Courage		
Fraud		
Love		
Deceit		
Cowardice		
Joy		
Fear		
Life purpose		
Spirit		
Business ethics		
Office politics		
Getting old		
Betrayal		
Clandestine sex		
Abuse of power		
Bullying at work		
Fulfilling your dreams		
Rivalry		
Rejection		
Inadequacy		
Loyalty		
Malice		
God's will		
Despair		
Fantasies		
Death		
Mental illness		
Ecstasy		
Redundancy		
Physical illness		
Opening up conflict		

0 = No difficulty; 1 = Slight difficuly; 2 = Moderate difficulty; 3 = Strong difficulty;
4 = No way.

Figure 4.1   Taboo areas questionnaire.

psychologically grounded approach for the experienced coach. Lloyd Denton's technique focuses particularly on leadership style. For another approach to leadership see *The leader's story* in the next section of this chapter. We were offered a third technique in this area, so it is clearly one of interest to contributors. The third activity was excluded as it was similar to Lloyd Denton's, but it focused particularly on permission to be powerful, and used the approach outlined in *Understanding leadership style*, focused around role models for the responsible use of power. We end this section with a provocative technique called *What is success?*

Challenging deeply held beliefs and assumptions
Sandra Henson, Ascentia

There are three core exercises I use to help clients challenge their assumptions and core beliefs. First, I explain the concept to clients, especially that people tend to make it hard for themselves to experience their *Moving towards values* and very easy to experience their *Moving away from values* (see Exercise 1 below). I need to gauge their interest in completing the exercise before sending it to them by email.

Clients are asked to complete the exercise as written below and during subsequent sessions we work on the values and rules – to check the order and whether any values are missing, and to examine the rules and how we can make it easier for them to experience what they want from life. This can be very exciting and illuminating work.

Then we look at the *Moving away from values* and rules. It can take clients a little while to appreciate the benefits. However, when the penny drops, the majority says it has been transformative and converts limiting rules to resourceful beliefs. Once we have a definitive set of values and rules the client often types these out on a single sheet of paper for frequent reference.

The other two exercises – 'Cost Benefit' and 'Belief Changing' – are used in client sessions if it appears relevant to do so. Unlike values and rules, we do these live. The examples given are the ones I share with clients to illustrate the process.

Exercise 1: Values and rules
This exercise will help you to identify your current most important values and to understand some of the current rules that you have in place to live by these values. It will help you understand your behaviour patterns better and then to shape these behaviours to better support you in achieving your goals.

Part 1: The first part of the exercise is for you to determine what are currently the 10–15 most important values to you in life. Examples might include *Achievement, Significance, Happiness, Growth* and *Freedom*. Please list or mind map the values.

Part 2: Next take the 10 most important values and rank them so that you generate your top ten, in their order of importance.

Part 3: Now list the rules that you associate with each value. Ask yourself the question 'What has to happen in order for me to feel ....(insert value)?'. An example of a rule would be *'For me to feel respected, people would have to listen to my point of view, take my opinion into account and solicit my views'*. Or, *'I receive recognition and validation every time someone honours me by sharing his or her experiences, thoughts or feelings'*.

Part 4: Many people have values which they are moving away from, such as rejection, failure and being embarrassed. Please list your top five moving-away-from values below. Use questions such as *'What are the feelings I would do almost anything to avoid having to feel?'*

Part 5: Now list the rules you currently have for your moving away from values. An example might be *'If I don't succeed the first time then I will have failed'* or *'I will never ever again indulge in the consistent experience of rejection as I always have something to contribute, whether expressed or not'*.

Well done, and thank you for completing this. Please bring it along to your next session where your coach will work with you based on the information you have provided.

Exercise 2: Cost–benefit exercise
This exercise will help you explore how holding certain beliefs can both benefit you and prevent you from changing aspects of your life.

It is part of a process to help you understand your current beliefs better and then for you to exercise choice on how you wish to move forward. The invitation is to work through the exercise using a particular deeply held belief.

Part 1: The first part of the exercise is for you to write down the current belief which you would like to change in the space below. An example might be *'I hate giving presentations'*.

Part 2: Now write down all the ways in which you are benefiting from holding this belief. It may seem strange to start with, though using the above as an example: *By holding this belief I avoid presentations which are stressful, I don't get worried, I avoid speaking out and drawing attention to myself, I avoid criticism, I avoid risking failure. I can stay in my comfort zone* etc. What would yours be?

Part 3: Now write down all the ways in which holding this belief costs you. Continuing with the above example, we could have: *It costs me promotion at work and achieving my career goals, the opportunity to grow, inner satisfaction, my financial ability to support the family; I am a poor role model for my children* etc.

Part 4: Now look at and write down the benefits if you were to change the belief. Many of these would be the opposite to Part 3 and it is worth writing these down. In addition you will find others. Continuing with the theme above, these could be: *I would be able to encourage and support my family; I would replace fear with relaxation and pleasure; I would gain respect from my peers; I would have fun; It would transform everything* etc.

Part 5: Now consider what the cost is really about. Examples are: *It is short term; it only requires an attitude shift; it's about taking first step* etc. What are the real costs to you?

Part 6: What would you like your new belief to be? Example: *I really enjoy presentations and every day I am getting more and more relaxed about them.* Take time to create your new belief.

Exercise 3: Belief changing exercise

This exercise will help you to understand the references you have built up to underpin certain beliefs, challenge them, and start the process of developing new references to take you towards your goals. When you have completed the exercise please forward your findings to your coach for your next session.

Phase I: Declaring your limiting belief.

First write down the limiting belief you have which you would like to change. This process can be carried out for most beliefs, though the recommendation is to go through the whole exercise with one belief at a time. An example might be: 'I am comfortable earning what I do and there is no need for me to earn more'.

Phase II: Write down all the references that underpin this belief.

You could imagine the belief as the surface of a table and all the references being the (many) table legs that support this belief. Examples might include: 'To earn more I would have to work longer hours'; 'I won't be able to give time to my family and friends (working too hard)'; 'I would have to become unacceptably political and compromise my values'; 'People won't like me, I won't be genuine'.

Phase III: Unpick the current references and replace them with ones that take you towards your goals.

Imagine taking the table apart and replacing the legs with new references. Continuing with the theme above, these could include: 'I need to work smarter, not harder'; 'Working smartly gives me more time with friends and family, not less'; 'I can choose to progress within a company and stick to my values'; 'My true friends like me for who I am, where the money is irrelevant'.

Phase IV: Replace the old limiting belief with a new one.

Write down the new belief that is underpinned by the references in Phase III. Continuing with the example, this could be 'There are an incredible number of ways for me to build my wealth'. What is yours?

Understanding leadership style

This approach, based upon the work of Warren Bennis, comes from Lloyd Denton, of Mentor-TR, Istanbul. It is a means of helping the learner reflect upon leadership style in general and their own leadership style in particular.

The coach/mentor first asks the learner to think of persons who have had a strong, positive influence on their career or personal development. Then she or he asks them to:

- Picture each individual and remember what they looked like and sounded like (this is often best done with the eyes closed).
- Describe in up to six words or phrases the qualities they most readily associate with this individual.
- Describe the feelings this individual stimulated in them (and whether the memory of the person still elicits those feelings).
- Think about the impact that person had upon their career, the choices they have made, the way that they think and so on.
- Define, if possible, where and how they used that person as a role model.
- Recall the limitations of that person (i.e. what were they a poor role model for? Did they fail you in any way?).
- Consider what price, if any, that person paid for the help they gave you.
- Consider whether how the learner acts towards others is affected by the way this person acted towards them.

This exploration of leadership in others provides a useful basis for developing an understanding of where the learner's leadership values and behaviours have come from and where some of the critical gaps might lie.

What is success?

The helper asks the learner to reflect for a few minutes on their personal criteria for success. Questions to ask include:

- What does success feel like to you?
- How would you know when you had got there?
- What evidence would you point to that indicates success for you?
- How will others regard you when you are successful?
- What about success in other areas of your life?

This can be confirming or clarifying for some, but others will be surprised that they can't articulate what success will look like, as in the case of Richard's coachee below.

Case study

Richard was an executive coach and he was working with Guy, a successful businessman, who wondered why everything seemed a burden, when it seemed he had nothing to worry about. Their conversation went as follows:

Richard: What are your goals for next year?
Guy: Next year I will become rich.
Richard: How much will you need to be rich?
Guy: Dunno.
Richard: How much did you make last year?
Guy: £4 million.
Richard: So how much more will you need to make this year?
Guy: Still don't know.

Guy is an extreme example of a condition that afflicts many of us. We have lots of 'on' buttons that get us going, but no 'off' buttons. Being clear about what success might mean is a first and essential step in discovering what is enough for a good life.

Bringing stereotypes into the open

Examine stereotypes from five perspectives:

- Those the mentor may hold about the mentee.
- Those the mentee may hold about the mentor.
- Those they may share about other people with whom the mentee has to interact.
- Those the mentee holds about him/herself that may hinder the achievement of relationship goals.
- Those the mentor holds about him/herself that may hinder the achievement of relationship goals.

How would you describe this *type* of person in terms of attributes you admire/ and those you dislike?

- What they typically do?
- What they typically say?
- How they say it?
- How they make you feel?
- What they think is important and unimportant at work and outside work? (Their defining beliefs.)

We offer two techniques for working on stereotypes: *The leader's story* focuses on leadership and *Issue mapping* is a more general one.

The leader's story

This simple technique for understanding culture and the executive's role within it is adapted from the Link&Learn Newsletter (15 November 2002). It has some similarities with career pathing (see Chapter 3). In the case quoted, the technique was used to develop a portfolio of leadership qualities to highlight corporate values. A coach/mentor might use the same approach to help an individual understand their own story and to compare their story with those of other people in the organization.

The executive is asked to look back upon his or her career and identify as many as possible of the highlights. Unlike career pathing, the highlights are more than just career decision points. They may include times when the executive felt extremely high or low, when they made big mistakes or scored significant successes against the odds, when they learned important lessons, when they encountered and built relationships with key people, when they had to take risks, and/or when they had to let go of things that were important to them.

These short narratives are time sequenced above, below or across a horizontal line that divides them into highs and lows (although some may be both). The coach–mentor explores these with the learner asking such questions as:

- How did you change as a result of this experience?
- What was the impact on others?
- Has your view of that experience changed over time?
- How will these experiences affect the decisions and behaviours you make in the future?
- How can you use these experiences to help others?
- What does this review of your story tell you about your values and what's important to you?
- Can you connect any part of your story to a challenge you currently face? That a colleague currently faces?

Issues mapping

Understanding the mixture of conflicting desires, constraints and drivers that operate on each of us is often difficult without help. Our inability to look at ourselves from the outside, or to listen carefully to what we say, will always be a limiting factor. One of the tools we have

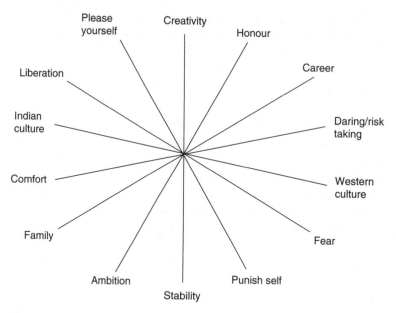

Figure 4.2   Issues mapping.

found to be invaluable in the early stages of a developmental relationship is issues mapping, which is a tool to enable the coach/mentor to reflect on how they see the learner, in terms of the dilemmas or inner conflicts they face.

At its core, the process is simply about listening: for recurring themes, for contradictions, for opposites, for patterns of almost any kind. Each time the coach/mentor identifies a theme, he draws it as a line, as illustrated in the diagram above. At each end of the line, the coach/mentor identifies a pair of competing demands upon the learner.

In this example, base d on a 90-minute initial meeting, the mentee was a young Asian woman who wanted to instil a sense of direction into her career. Now in her early thirties and single, she lived at home, as is customary among families from India and Pakistan. The conflicts she experienced emanated in large part from the conflict between the culture of her family and that of the broader society in which she lived and worked. Having a career had become very important to her in recent years, but she also felt the need to settle down and have a family. Many of the jobs she would like to do, which carried greater responsibility, would be regarded by her family and community as unsuitable, because, for example, they involved travelling and staying in hotels alone. Living at home was comfortable and inexpensive, but it constrained her in many ways that she found insufferable. Leaving home (liberation) was an option, even though it would cause great arguments with her father and mother, and she feared losing their trust and approval. Staying in the same job, even thought it did not pay well, avoided confronting issues, but she had long outgrown it and wanted the chance to use her creative mind on bigger work tasks. She fluctuated between periods of rebellion (please yourself) and submissive guilt (punish yourself).

Having agreed with her that these were all valid conflicts for her ('Nobody has ever summed me up so succinctly'), the mentor asked her to consider what compromises she had made in each case. For example, she would wear traditional dress at home and at community events, but Western clothes at work or when she went out with girl friends. *How happy was she with each of the compromises? Which ones would she like to change, and how?* Within a short space of time, she identified a number of decisions she had to make, if she were to take greater charge of her life and career. These then became the topics for the next mentoring session.

Understanding one's life and career

One of the central tasks of mentoring is to help people bring their lives into focus. Sometimes this focus is directed at the whole of the mentee's life; on other occasions it is more narrowly directed at their career. We give below techniques related to each of these perspectives. Stories can be individuals' own autobiographies, which can be factual (see *My story*) or crafted into a fiction (see Julie Allan's *Using fictional stories in coaching*). For a full account of the use of creative writing in development and in therapy, see Bolton (2001) and Bolton *et al.* (2004).

My story

This is a technique that can be used at various levels of mentoring and coaching dialogue. The aim is to help learners gain a broader and more insightful perspective on themselves.

The task set for them is to write – over a week or two in most cases – *my story, past present and future*. Like any good story, the story of me has multiple dimensions and a large part of the value of the exercise is for the learner to revisit what they have written and add or amend over a period. Re-reading my story 6 months or more after it was written can be a deeply affecting experience; it also helps the individual recognize how much they have learned.

In constructing *my story*, the learner needs to be directed not just to write a CV or mini-biography. A story is very different from a report. It has, among other elements:

- A plot.
- Several sub-plots.
- A cast of supporting characters.
- A backcloth (the environment, place and society where the story unfolds).
- A moral (or perhaps several).
- Choices and dilemmas.
- Drama – deep disappointments and triumphs.
- A sense of continuity – grand themes that are echoed as the story unfolds.

Exploring the past in this way provides insights into motivations, fears, aspirations and forgotten dreams. Because the story demands that these be related to the present, it helps the learner understand more clearly *How and why did I get to be me?* and to consider how they feel about who and where they are.

Writing *my story* into the future is often the most difficult, but a deeper understanding of the past and present helps the learner choose what they really want and visualize who and where they want to be. Tapping into their grand themes is a very powerful source of self-motivation.

The role for the coach or mentor is first to encourage the learner to write their story. Especially if the person is not used to writing at length (or only used to writing reports), they may need some encouragement first – perhaps by beginning the story verbally, with the helper as the audience. The second role for the coach–mentor is to help the learner recognize and explore the plots, moral and grand themes, so that they develop deeper understanding.

My story has been used to help people make fundamental changes in their ambitions, in their behaviours and in their lives in general. It is, in our view, one of the most powerful techniques in the coach–mentor's toolbag.

Using fictional stories in coaching
Julie Allan

There are a number of complementary ways in which stories may be useful in a coaching context. The stories can be offered by the coach or by the coachee, and they may be true-to-life or fictional. Here we look at the use of fictional stories to help illuminate workplace situations.

The use of narratives in psychology has a long history, centred around the quest for insight into human behaviour – either our own or other people's. And an important aspect of this quest is to gain understanding of the ways in which we 'sense-make', or make meaning from our lives. Story-telling is in an evident relationship with this endeavour and has in some way been addressed by theorists from a variety of disciplines including psychology, anthropology and organizational behaviour. For example, the personal construct psychology of Kelly (1955), addresses our ways of 'construing' ourselves in relation to the world – we act in accordance with, and perhaps even become, the story we tell about 'how things are'. Bruner (1990) also looks at meaning-making. McAdams (1993) has also addressed the concept of people as being the stories they tell (rather than simply telling stories). Jung's archetypes (Fordham, 1991 is a useful introduction), Berne's Transactional Analysis scripts (1975) and Bettelheim's well-known work (1991) on the role of stories and tales in our lives, all speak to different aspects of story in our lives. Weick, in particular, drew on the work of both psychologists and organizational theorists to illuminate his position in *Sensemaking in Organisations* (1995).

When using fictional stories in coaching, the intention is to encourage some playful and creative thought about a situation, using metaphor and analogy as a bridge that can:

- help connect aspects of the current situation with existing experiences and understanding;
- Help steping out of the situation and taking a 'view from the side';
- Engage creative thought and new connections.

Case study Stuart

Stuart is a 34-year-old departmental head of a large charity. He works his socks off. He's regarded as successful and has been using coaching to take an appreciative enquiry stance towards his own work and towards the development of those who work for him. His 'people management' capabilities were what he felt needed some attention.

At one session, he raised a new issue. His own line manager was generally quite remote, and Stuart was becoming dissatisfied. He kept this man updated through a variety of reports but felt his manager didn't share his concern for what he believed to be key areas of the business. He had drafted a memo thanking his manager for his response to previous reports – a response which had not been forthcoming. He wanted advice from his coach on whether it was appropriate.

(Continued)

Now, there are many questions which might arise from this situation, including, 'Does your line manager want or need those reports?' and 'What result do you wish to achieve?' With Stuart's permission, the coach used a story approach.

The coach gave Stuart an invitation. 'Take some time just to let your mind wander and seek out a fictional story, or a story character, that you think has something in common with your situation. It doesn't have to be an exact match. And it can be any kind of fictional story, old or new'.

Stuart quickly cast himself in the role of 'the train who can'. As he spoke about his choice, he came to the conclusion that the organization was full of 'trains who can'. In childhood, he'd understood the tale to be all about persevering and, therefore, succeeding – which was a good thing. And he'd been doing it ever since. But in relation to his current situation, he felt like 'the train who can't'.

'Why can't the train this time?' asked the coach.

'Because I'm not a bloody train!' came the reply.

'Let's find a fictional character you can be instead'.

'Luke Skywalker. Did you know there's a website where you can fill in a questionnaire and find out which Star Wars character you are? I'm Luke Skywalker'.

'OK, so what would Luke do?'

'Luke would keep fighting for the side of good. My director isn't Darth, he's more of a Wookie – on my side but I think speaking a different language. Luke would know Wookie, or would know somebody who did'.

And so, Stuart's personal hero engaged with the task. With his need to keep going up the same steep hill at all costs abandoned, he went off to research a more useful and effective communication method.

Application

It's helpful in using this approach if the coach is reasonably versed in some of the psychological theories connected with the use of stories. However, the use proposed here is not the same as approaches that may be taken by professionals with a clinical population. Rather, it is a way of engaging what people can do through the use of metaphor. Curious and appreciative questioning will help the coachee illuminate their own tale and is complementary to the use of other approaches, including a focus on goal-setting, for example. It functions 'by invitation only'. Imposing this way of working with somebody who it doesn't suit can lead to de-skilling of the individual.

In this way of working, it is important that the coachee should choose their own tales. However, there are circumstances under which a tale or

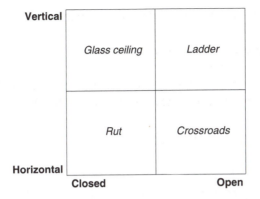

Figure 4.3   Map of career metaphors.

character can be offered by the coach. Again, this is 'by invitation only' and if appropriate to the particular coaching relationship. For example, 'When you tell me about that situation, it makes me think of those stories in which something is not as it seems, like Red Riding Hood and her grandmother', or, 'I'm getting a sense that lots of things flew out of Pandora's box and the lid got slammed shut on Hope....' Such comments help invite dialogue and exploration and are useful as exploratory comments on the dynamics of a situation rather than for labelling. Diagnoses such as, 'You're quite right, Jack's behaving just like Zeus and throwing thunderbolts around', may not be productive.

A final point. European fairy tales and Greek myths have currency in many circles – various authors have addressed aspects of Greek myth or Shakespearean characters in organizational settings. But there is a vast depth and breadth of stories available from every culture, and this is another reason why the coachee's choice of metaphor should be respected. Perhaps Kali, or Sita and Rama, or Anansi, or Coyote are the characters who have most to offer. In the end, all problems can start to look like a hut on hen's legs, if Baba Yaga is your only tool.

Career metaphor

Coaches and mentors can ask the people they are working with to think up a metaphor to describe their career. The metaphor may be about anything that is vivid for the learner, whether it is a football team, a string quartet, a car or a movie.

This metaphor may be linked to a map of career metaphors. Figure 4.3 shows that metaphors can be seen as either horizontal or vertical, and either open or closed.

The coach can then ask questions along the lines of:

- Which of these quadrants do you see your own career as being in at present?
- Are there other quadrants that appear more attractive?
- What do you need to do that will help you to move positions within this map?

References

Anderson, W. (1996). *The Face of Glory: Creativity, Consciousness and Civilization*. London: Bloomsbury.

Berne, E. (1975). *What Do You Say After You Say Hello?* London: Corgi/ Transworld.

Bettelheim, B. (1991). *The Uses of Enchantment*. London: Penguin.

Bolton, G. (2001). *Reflective Practice: Writing and Professional Development*. London: Paul Chapman.

Bolton, G., Howlett, S., Lago, C. and Wright, J. K. (2004). *Writing Cures: An Introductory Handbook of Writing in Counselling and Psychotherapy*. Hove: Brunner-Routledge.

Bruner, J. (1990). *Acts of Meaning*. London: Harvard University Press.

Fordham, F. (1991). *An Introduction to Jung's Psychology*. Harmondsworth: Penguin.

Grayling, A. C. (2004). *What is Good?* London: Orion.

Kelly, G. A. (1955). *The Psychology of Personal Constructs*, Vols 1 and 2. New York: W W Norton.

McAdams, D. P. (1993). *The Stories We Live By*. New York and London: Guilford Press.

Weick, K. E. (1995). *Sensemaking in Organisations*. London: Sage

Whitworth, L., Kimsey House, H. and Sandhal, P. (1998). *Co-Active Coaching*. Palo Alto, CA: Davies-Black.

Chapter 5

Understanding other people's behaviour

Introduction

We would like to focus upon two aspects to understanding others – one is helping the mentee/coachee to understand third parties and the other is the especial challenge of empathizing in the coaching/mentoring relationship with those who are different from us.

Understanding others seems to be a key part of what our coachees/ mentees want or need from our work with them. We find that often this issue merges with the player understanding him- or herself (see Chapter 4). Empathy as a quality of the coachee to develop is little discussed in the coaching literature (it was not mentioned in the index of most of the texts listed in Part 3). Where it was mentioned (McLeod, 2003, pp. 173–74), it was seen as a problem, in that empathic projection could lead coaches to assume that their coachees' feelings were the same as their own. Nonetheless, we feel that empathic understanding of others is an important topic and techniques for this are addressed in the next section. The technique *Focus for change* illustrates the ambiguity between understanding self and understanding others. *Using 'heightened intuition'* is a technique from the wild side for developing this empathy.

The second aspect of bridging difference is strikingly described by Eileen Murphy in her work with school children, using *A solution focused approach*. Amarjeet Rebolo describes techniques to break *Cycles of oppression*. Beery and Jicheva describe their online approach, *Argonaut – a tool for coaching across cultures*, and give a vivid case study of developing intercultural understanding. Zulfi Hussein describes his approach to

Mentoring across cultures, and we end this chapter with a technique for *Questioning assumptions and stereotypes*.

Empathy for others

Focus for change

One of the big issues in coaching is to decide what it is that the coachee will focus upon and change. As coaches we can work with people at a number of levels:

- Changing the environment
- Changing the organization
- Changing a team
- Changing another individual
- Changing oneself.

For each of these levels we can attend to the following:

- Changing values and beliefs
- Changing attitudes
- Changing behaviours
- Changing thoughts/opinions.

All these levels are legitimate foci of concern. However, in helping coachees to navigate among these options, it is well to remember two principles:

1. There is a strong argument for starting with oneself (see Cecilia case study below).
2. If someone changes behaviour and maintains the change for a month, then attitudes, and even values and beliefs are likely to follow; sometimes it is necessary to change thoughts in order to be able to change behaviours (see Margot case study below).

> **Case study**   **Cecilia coaches Alex**
>
> The coach Cecilia was a senior HR person who was helping a colleague manage her career. The colleague, Alex, had a sombre style of self-presentation, but was otherwise highly effective in analysing issues, making plans, delivering to target and so on. However, this style was seen as off-putting by many

in the senior management team and when Alex came up for promotion they made it clear that they did not want such a grumpy-seeming person on the team.

Cecilia wondered whether the issue was about whether to change the person or to change impressions of the person among the senior team.

During a supervision session, Cecilia came to realize that she had lots of attitudes of her own to Alex which would stand in the way of being able dispassionately to help her, so the first step was to work on the coach's own attitudes and behaviours. Having done this in supervision, Cecilia was able to help Alex focus on *herself*.

Case study   Margot

The coachee, Margot, was a director of a function of the European subsidiary of a global company, with HQ in the USA. She was dispirited and resentful about having set up a programme in Europe and then hearing that there was going to be a conference call at convenient American times to decide on the global approach to the issue. Initially Margot was not even invited to join the conference. She felt that all her good work would come to naught as the custom in the company was that the US way of doing things became adopted as the global template.

During coaching, Margot was asked what state she was in. She replied that she was falling into a victim state. She was asked what state she thought would be most effective in getting what she wanted. She replied, 'A sales state'. She then explored what someone in such a state would be prepared to do. She decide that, if push came to shove, a determined sales state would lead her to take the issue right up to the global chief operating officer, if necessary.

As it turned out, this was not necessary, because the tele-conference accepted her enthusiastic presentation of the European way and that was adopted as a global standard.

Using 'heightened intuition'

In his book, *The Sense of Being Stared At*, Rupert Sheldrake refers to the phenomenon experienced by many psychotherapists, wherein communication between professional and client appears to be telepathic. Sheldrake's analysis of this link attempts to integrate, rather than separate, the concept of extended mind link with the instinctive and unconscious clues that pass between people.

The circumstances in which such scientifically inexplicable (within the context of any testable theory) communication occurs, seem to be most frequent among people who have established a strong emotional bond over time. For example, Sheldrake observes that mothers who breastfeed for longer are more likely to report intuitive and premonitive lactation. He points out that Sigmund Freud documented and personally experienced inexplicable moments of apparent telepathy with clients/subjects.

Coaches and mentors may also develop strong empathy. Allowing this empathy to develop into what we might call *heightened intuition* is potentially useful in developing insight and modifying questioning approaches to the learner. (To use the term telepathy might imply a rather more complete form of communication.)

The keys to letting heightened intuition occur appear to be the following:

- Accept that a 'meeting of minds' is feasible and relatively commonplace.
- Attempt to 'listen' to the learner's concerns during the salient spaces; imagine you are able to share their feelings and visualizations.
- Use language that draws upon any impressions you receive and observe whether they strike a chord.
- Rather than offer a solution to a problem, visualize it strongly in your own mind and try to 'send' the visualization to the learner.
- If they appear to have caught the visualization, follow through with questions that explore what they understood and what it means for them.
- Don't expect to intuit what the other person is thinking – or have them intuit what you have in your mind – more than occasionally. All you are trying to do is use your natural empathetic and other senses to increase your 'hit' rate.
- Don't get all mystical and try to explain the transfer of ideas. Just accept that it happened, that it could be coincidence, or entirely a matter of unconscious and subtle hints and that it has been helpful to the learner!

Bridging difference

A solution focused approach
Eileen Murphy

The solution focused approach offers simple, effective tools that allow the mentee's own voice to be heard and for the setting of small, identified goals towards change.

Many people who experience difficulty often become isolated and develop negative views of themselves and others; the language of the approach helps us to introduce an element of questioning of this negative and destructive view.

The solution focused approach is a model that focuses on people's **competencies** rather than their deficits, their **strengths** rather than their weaknesses, their **possibilities** rather than their limitations.

The mentor validates the client's views, searches for times when they are different, then investigates what's different at those times, allowing the client to hear in real ways how they affect situations, positively and negatively.

The fundamental principles of the approach are that the individual is the expert in how they react to situations, in what works best for them and in what doesn't work. The mentor's role is to elicit that information by asking useful and creative questions.

The solution focused mentor is 'curious' rather than 'prescriptive', asking 'How will you deal with this?', rather than, 'This is what I think you should do', because individuals learn more about themselves when their opinions are asked.

Reframing

Reframing is a common therapeutic tool – taking a negative word and putting a less negative meaning to it. This is not to minimize the problem, and it is important that people don't feel that their opinions are not valid.

Reframing suggests a new and different way of behaving, freeing the client to alter behaviour and making it possible to bring about changes, while 'saving face.'

For instance, a person who has been labelled as 'lazy' is often trapped in that image. Reframing the word to 'laid back' often allows for the start of a journey towards 'more energetic', for instance, 'I got the impression from what has been said that you were quite laid back in that particular lesson' – leading to 'If the teacher said you were more energetic in class, what would you be doing differently?'

Similarly with other labels that young people are often given or use about others:

DISTRACTED......................interested in lots of things
IMPATIENT...........................action orientated, has a high standard
UNCARING..........................detached
DEPRESSED.........................overwhelmed, taking time out
AGGRESSIVE.......................forceful
NAGGING............................shows concern, trying to bring out best
STUBBORN..........................determined, self-willed
TALKS TO MUCH................communicator, expressive
DYSLEXIC............................has a different way of learning

Exceptions

Exceptions can often trigger strengths that have long been forgotten.

For instance, following the reframing exercise of 'lazy' to 'laid back', and asking about the 'energetic' difference, the mentor might then ask questions about times when they *have* been 'energetic' in a class or group, and what they were doing differently, what difference that made to them and what difference it made to others.

The mentor uses, WHAT, WHERE, WHEN, WHO and HOW questions rather than FEELING questions in order for the changes to be observable to both client and helper.

'What will you be doing that will tell others that you are *switched on*?'
'What difference will this make to you?'
'Where will it matter most?'

Once 'observable actions' have been established, the helper can give small tasks around these actions to be reviewed at the next session.

Sometimes, just asking about exceptions to difficulties can be helpful to a person, because it is a reality that people don't often have the emotional sophistication to sit down and reflect on times when they have coped with similar problems, and therefore remind themselves that they are capable of dealing with difficulties.

The mentor can be very effective in raising the young person's awareness of their strengths simply by asking subtle questions about exceptions.

Equally, exceptions can highlight how the person's behaviour affects situations positively and negatively.

Future talk

Future talk is a form of visualization that is helpful in mentoring. It allows clients to identify small, observable, achievable tasks that would bring about change in a difficulty they are facing, whether it is a small difficulty, e.g. they feel left out of a group, or a bigger problem such as they don't have enough confidence to engage in an activity, or they may lack support at a meeting where they will be asked to address inappropriate behaviour.

It encourages all to hear a point of view that they many not have heard before and, because it does not involve 'blaming', it allows others involved to hear their part in the change process.

'If I met you next week and you were in control of things and were doing OK, and I asked you how it had happened – who had done what – what would you be telling me?'

- What's happening differently now that you are doing OK?
- How do you control things?
- How do you cope *now* when you feel frustrated – what do you do?
- If I saw you the day after things started changing, what would I have noticed that was different?

- What would others be doing differently?
- How are people different with you – what are they saying/doing differently?

Once you have established what they understand as needing to be done differently, setting an observation task or monitor chart for them is useful. For example, 'because you said that doing this would make a difference to your behaviour, I would like you to observe what difference it makes in the next week.'

Bridging difference

Cycle of oppression
Amarjeet Rebolo

In Western society, white people have the ultimate power and non-whites and ethnic minorities have less power. Individuals, organizations and society see the black and ethnic minorities as powerless individuals/ groups. Assumptions are made about them. They are often given negative labels. These names can be internalized by them so they start thinking like the label. Thinking can then develop into negative behaviour. And so the cycle continues.

Empowerment
The cycle of oppression can be broken down slowly by empowering individuals, by giving them information, training or education.

As human beings, they have been put on this earth for a reason. They have rights under varied equality Acts, policies and procedures (depending on where they are based). Learning can give the power of knowledge to challenge individuals to assert their rights. Explaining how the mind works and how accelerated learning can help them in any learning in life can help. These two things are often very enlightening and empowering for the individual.

When they are called negative names by anyone they can do the following:

- Stop and acknowledge their feelings and challenge the individuals with questions; how, why or what (if they are able to do so).
- Encourage the person to pick easy challenges at first, and progress slowly to more difficult situations.
- Role-play a key situation to gain confidence.
- Learn to stop, listen to their feelings, acknowledge, and try to release them. The more this is done the better one feels.

In order to avoid internalizing negative responses, encourage the learner to use affirmations regularly if possible, to put them in strategic places. Also use problem-solving to develop strategies for different situations. Then monitor by keeping a diary or journal to check on reality and balance their perspective.

These approaches can be used in:

● cross-cultural work
● age – young or older
● gender issues
● disabilities issues.

Further details can be found in LGMB/ILGS (1991).

Examples of its use

I have used it with adults and children of varied age; in men and women from different cultures here and from abroad, in community, voluntary, and statutory organizations. I have not found it helpful with white men.

Issues and observations to consider:

● Best way this individual learns.
● Their level of understanding.
● Their beliefs/values.
● The emotions they may be experiencing.
● Type of problems they may be having.
● Their wider support network.

Argonaut – a tool for coaching across cultures
Caroline Beery and Maria Jicheva

This technique uses a tool that is available from Coghill and Beery (www.coghillberry.com), but can be adapted in part with frameworks from the literature (e.g. Rosinski, 2003) or from your own experience.

Perceptions create reality – and, is that enough? Often coachees have very little knowledge of their selected target culture or, if they have some experience, it can be filtered through the eyes of others who have a very different set of lenses. And, more importantly, they may have limited self-awareness as to how they are perceived by others. In order for coachees to receive feedback beyond their perceptions, Argonaut provides a 'reality check' for the user's target culture. The reality check is a generalized description of the culture based on research and reading.

The 'reality check' provides coachees with one more data point for helping them understand themselves and other cultures. Each perceptual level – self, home and target – can be mapped on to the 'reality check.'

Intercultural coaching

Coaching across borders is a special challenge. Before a coaching plan can be put in place, client and coach need to understand the client's cultural assumptions and values, and the values and orientations of the cultures with whom they work. Once they have a clearer awareness of their cultural lenses (such as their need for a closely scheduled timetable, or their understanding that their communication style is not clear to those from other cultures), they can begin to make progress towards achieving their goals.

The Argonaut map

This is a web-based tool. Coachees complete 36 questions rating themselves on a scale from 1 to 7, on three different levels: (1) how I perceive myself, (2) how I perceive my home culture, and (3) how I perceive the target culture.

Case study   **Robert works in Bulgaria**

Robert was working on a really interesting project in Bulgaria. Not that it was his favourite part of the world, yet the people were nice and it turned out to be true that they did not export their best wine. That was his second project in Bulgaria. The first time he had a Spanish colleague on his team and despite the slow pace at which things happened, the project was successfully completed. But this time... .

He was becoming increasingly aware that, despite his expectations of things running more smoothly (the Spaniard wasn't there to slow things down), they had almost come to a halt. This is how we met. Robert needed to understand what was stopping him from achieving his goals.

We asked him to complete Argonaut, a web-based 20-minute cultural assessment. It created a personal cultural map of Robert's preferences and invited him to map his perceptions of Bulgarian culture. Robert positioned Bulgaria very close to his own profile. He did not see many differences between the way he did things and the way in which his Bulgarian counterparts operated. The only significant difference was in the way they used time – they seemed to see it as a never-ending resource that they could flexibly expand when needed.

We had a long discussion on what the strategies of adapting to a more flexible style of treating time would be. He came up with a long list:

- Build 'slack time' into a timetable.
- Be prepared to move to new challenges before completing earlier ones.

(Continued)

- May need to proceed to the next issue before achieving clarity on the one being discussed. The new information will enrich the whole picture and help the solution.

We discussed the next business deal he was to have in Bulgaria and practised several ways to shift the way he communicated with his team-mates and customers.

The next conversation took place when he returned from Bulgaria. He described what he said and did, the effect it had on the transactions and how he felt. Though it was difficult for him to be set a realistic deadline and to be very clear and direct in giving orders, he made an effort. Robert thought that he made a breakthrough as he felt more in control of the situation. As he said, 'At least now I understand what is going on'.

Learning to work and live across cultures is an interactive process. You become aware, you try out some new responses, you analyse these, you tweak them, you learn something new, you try another approach. There is no immediate 'right' answer. It is an exciting process to coach individuals and teams who may be highly educated and experienced, yet, with one intercultural encounter, can give the impression that they have returned to nursery school.

With the help of tools such as Argonaut, which makes virtual coaching a possibility, an intercultural novice can gain important self-knowledge and cultural understanding for moving up the ladder to 'unconscious competence.'

When compared to Robert's perceived understanding of target culture, it was clear there might be issues other than just 'time spans' to address. This is the starting point for asking more questions to learn about Robert's self-awareness, his perceptual abilities, his ability to empathize and read body language, his flexibility in solving problems and his adaptability in general.

I began by asking Robert on what he based his perceptions of Bulgaria and Bulgarians. Since he had had experience working in the country and with a multinational team, he had good critical incidents on which to draw, which I asked him to describe.

Argonaut also has the ability to compare two cultures different from self and target. You remember that Robert had had a Spaniard on his team as well. I asked him to compare the Spanish–Bulgarian profiles to gain insight into the ways the Spanish and Bulgarians would work together. He also then wanted to explore his own English culture in comparison to the Spanish. Once he had a sense of his own personal values, orientations and communication style, we discussed the effect of his personal and cultural style on the people with whom he conducts business internationally.

The 36 questions cluster along 12 dimensions. These are the significant cultural dimensions from our research that create the greatest challenges or conundrums for individuals living and working multinationally. The dimensions on Argonaut are:

- Time spans
- Use of time
- Group membership
- Power
- Rules
- Responsibility
- Tasks
- Problem-solving
- Space
- Fate
- Communication
- Conflict.

Once Robert completed his assessment, his answers were compiled and his results displayed in 12 sectors of a circle. At that point, he can compare his perceptions of: self and home, self and target, and home and target.

Robert's perception is that in the dimension of 'time spans', he perceives the greatest conflicts. At that point he visited that dimension and reviewed it in greater depth. The fields available to him are: 'strategies for dealing with difference', 'more about the target culture', 'more about my culture' and 'suggestions for resolving dilemmas'. These perceptual differences are the starting point of the coaching conversation. 'Time spans' may become an area of coaching focus for Robert if he feels (as he clearly does), it is important to make further investigations in order to reach his goals.

'Reality check'

As we were working together at our computers – Robert was in his office in Leeds and I was in London – we went to the 'reality check' area of Argonaut. By pressing a button we started comparing Robert's profile to the group profiles of all the Bulgarians we had on the database. The 'radiating signals' were now pulsating in new areas: task/relationship, group orientation, responsibility, and direct/indirect style of communicating. These were areas in which he thought he was doing OK, yet after analysing his recent experience he started linking some of the problems he was experiencing with these particular areas of cultural difference.

Coaching is about unleashing people's potential and helping them achieve their goals. In our polyphonic, multicultural world, it is often cultural differences that get in the way. The first step to overcome the cultural 'hurdle' is self-awareness: How do I perceive myself? How do I do things? How do I perceive the people who see me? How do people perceive me and what can I do to leverage the differences?

Mentoring across cultures
Zulfi Hussein

A good analogy to mentoring is the 'life cycle' of an acorn. Visualizing the mentee as an acorn being given the right quantities of coaching and feedback in a healthy non-judgemental environment, they will take root and start to blossom until they reach the maturity of a great tree. They will then go on to produce lots more acorns, which, in turn, will repeat the cycle.

Helping individuals to realize their full potential is what mentoring is about. For mentoring to have a positive outcome, mentors need to have a particular set of communication skills that they are able to use when interacting with their mentees. These skills include the ability to ask deep meaningful questions, listen actively and provide constructive feedback.

In addition, if mentors are to work with individuals from other cultures then they require an additional set of skills. In order to mentor a person from a different culture, the mentor needs to be able to determine how their own culture and the culture of their mentees will impact their communication. This is of key importance not only in the context of mentoring, but in all types of communication across cultures.

For mentors to be effective across cultures they must be culturally literate and be sensitive to the needs of individuals from different cultural backgrounds. Having cultural literacy means that one understands the values, beliefs and symbols of the dominant culture and how they are reflected in assumptions and behaviours. It also means one understands the values, beliefs and symbols of other cultures and how they too are reflected in a set of assumptions and behaviours. The mentors must also understand the values, beliefs and symbols of the organization that are reflected in the employees' assumptions and behaviours.

Cross-cultural mentoring provides an ideal opportunity to enhance the understanding of different cultures for both mentors and mentees. It also promotes learning for both partners on how to communicate across cultures.

Mentors and mentees need to accept and appreciate differences for the relationship to be most effective. This can be done by:

- acknowledging that cultural differences exist;
- being open to understanding cultural differences;
- recognizing that there is more that one way of looking at and doing things;
- handling differences with respect and sensitivity.

Mentoring can be promoted across cultures by:

- helping employees understand and appreciate diversity;
- extending personal and professional development opportunities to all employees;

● ensuring that the organizational environment supports rather than hinders cross-cultural communication.

> ## Case study   Zulfi's experience
>
> As a mentor I have used a combination of good questioning, active listening and constructive feedback skills to help people from different backgrounds reach their full potential. However, I have found that there is a real need to have a good understanding of the different cultures that come into play in a mentoring relationship (e.g. my culture, the mentee's culture and the culture of the organization) and their potential impact on communication. I have often had to adjust my style to suit the needs of the mentee. For example, I have not expected the same level of eye contact from a young Muslim female as from a young English female because I know that the young Muslim female will avoid lots of eye contact as a sign of respect. I have also had to take account of the fact that an African male may well make more use of his hands and arms, which could be perceived by some as being aggressive.
>
> Although it has taken me some time to develop cultural literacy through research and practice, I have found this to be an invaluable asset when mentoring across cultures. It has helped me quickly develop sustainable and highly effective mentoring relationships, which has lead to a great deal of mutual learning and growth.

Questioning assumptions and stereotypes

Particularly in mentoring relationships within diversity management programmes, people can find it difficult to identify and deal with stereotypes. A useful exercise to make the topic less threatening and to develop the skills of exploring stereotypes is for both mentor and mentee to reveal three or more assumptions that they have made about the other person.

Having shared the assumptions, the pair explore (a) how accurate or not they were and (b) how they arrived at the assumption in the first place. For example:

● You must have a very tidy home (because you wear a lot of jewellery and take care of your appearance).
● You are a very passionate person (you wear large red beads).
● You drive a red sports car (because you are highly extrovert).

Working through the chain of logic and association helps the learner understand how they come to conclusions about other people. The dangers and benefits of using stereotypes also come into clearer focus. After a few sessions, mentor and mentee typically become quite comfortable with saying to each other, 'My assumption is that you.... How accurate is that?'

References

Local Government Management Board/Institute of Local Government Studies (1991). *Quality and Equality: Service to the Whole Community*. Birmingham: Birmingham University.

McLeod, A. (2003). *Performance Coaching: The Handbook for Managers, H. R. Professionals and Coaches*. Bancyfelin, Carmarthen: Crown House.

Rosinski, P. (2003). *Coaching Across Cultures*. London: Nicholas Brealey.

Chapter 6

Dealing with roadblocks

Introduction

One of the great unanswerable questions we face as coaches is, 'What aspects of themselves can people change, and what can't they change?' Then, within the body of things that they can change there lie those things that they might change but which might have undesirable effects and would thus be best left as they are. These matters are not often discussed in coaching manuals, where the flexibility and 'improvability' of humankind is often taken for granted.

We are inclined to take a more circumspect approach. We say, 'Let's look all the way round the issue before deciding to plunge enthusiastically ahead'. When one of the authors finds himself stuck behind a slow-moving vehicle if in a hurry to get somewhere, we sometimes refer to the roadblock as an 'angel'. By being there the angelic hindrance may well prevent a speeding fine or even an accident. Not all blocks are pernicious.

So the first step in the process of dealing with roadblocks is to *identify* them. Then we need to decide what we want to do with them – *respect* them (nearly always), *live with* them, or *move* them. We offer a range of techniques that address these aspects of roadblocks.

Identifying roadblocks

Many helpees do not know what it is that (for example) prevents them from achieving more or being valued and respected. The smarter and the more successful they are, the harder it seems to be for them to identify the blocks (Argyris, 1991). Various psychological mechanisms seem to contribute to this difficulty, particularly projection, which involves imputing to others qualities that are one's own (Lee, 2003, p. 46).

Facing our own monsters

Coachees often have strengths which they carry to excess – where persistence becomes aggression or achievement orientation becomes competitiveness. Because they have relied on a particular strength for their success, they can be reluctant to acknowledge the down-side of the quality.

Case study   James

James is a director of a high-profile body that provides a range of services to the public. He feels that he does not get credit for his achievements because the other members of the executive of his organization are fiercely competitive. He sees them as stealing the credit that rightly belongs to him. He just wants – according to his own account – to have an atmosphere of plain dealing and honesty. However, he also talks about having to go behind their backs to the chief executive to gain the recognition that he deserves. He seems to outsiders, including his coach, to be fiercely competitive, but, when challenged, he explicitly denies this. It is only once he comes to terms with this competitive spirit inside himself that he can use his candour and goodwill to challenge the dysfunctional dynamics within the executive board of the organization.

Deciding what to do with roadblocks – respecting them

Layers of change

Part of respect is to recognize different impulses within us. The two techniques here represent two dimensions of this – the *Layers of change* technique looks at increasing depth of self and corresponding difficulty of change. The *Separate selves* technique looks at horizontal differences in ourselves – where we have impulses in two contrary directions at the same time.

Opinions
⇧
Attitudes
⇧
Behaviour
⇧
Personality
⇧
Temperament

Figure 6.1   Layers of the self.

One way of thinking about ourselves is as a series of layers of self, where each succeeding layer is fed and shaped by the layer above. So, for example, we may see ourselves as having the following layers in Figure 6.1.

So, according to this model, it is easiest to change our opinions and most difficult to change our temperament; in fact, it is not difficult – it is impossible.

Case study   Paul

Paul is the youngest member of a team, and also the fattest. He gets a certain amount of 'good-natured' ribbing from his colleagues about this, which eventually impels him to try the Atkins diet. This works for him and he both loses weight and feels more energetic. Fortified by this success, he decides to work with a naïve and optimistic coach on his introversion. Everything they try leaves him with a sense of failure. This is accurate: he has failed. Not for lack of application, but because he is attempting to change something – a core personality attribute – which is, according to mainstream psychology (Persaud, 2001, pp. 291–92), pretty well unchangeable. There are behaviours associated with introversion that he might be able to change but the deep-seated preference for looking inside and being energized by this is built into how he is and he is not therefore a suitable subject for coaching.

Separate selves

Separate selves is a simple but practical tool for helping people understand the complexity of their own thinking and to move into concerted action. In recent years, the notion of a single personality for each person has been questioned in the light of contrary evidence. Whatever the truth of that debate, it is clear that people often have a different set of perceptions, responses and attitudes in different situations. At its simplest, this may be seen in the difference in the voice tone, body posture and manner of someone on the telephone compared with how they would speak face to face; this is seen at its strongest among generations who grew up without universal personal telephone access, giving the appearance that they have 'become a different person'. Other examples might be how someone behaves at work, versus at home; or being subdued and withdrawn in the company of strangers, yet the life and soul of the party among close friends.

These differences in response are not always obvious to the person concerned. Separate selves invites the learner to observe consciously their different expressions of personality. For example:

- Your optimistic self vs. your pessimistic self
- Your active/assertive self vs. your passive self

- Your adventurous self vs. your cautious self
- Your serious self vs. your fun self
- Your private self vs. your public self.

Standard psychometrics, such as the Myers Briggs Type Indicator (MBTI) can also be a rich source of behavioural opposites. For example, in MBTI terms, one of the authors of this book (you can guess which!) is an ENTJ (extrovert, intuitive, thinking, judgemental). In certain situations, however, the introvert side of his nature emerges strongly – he greatly enjoys long, solitary walks, for example, where he can examine his inner perceptions. In others, he becomes highly perceptive – learning by experimenting and avoiding set solutions. Understanding the range of one's situational behaviours is highly beneficial in developing alternative solutions to issues.

From the initial discussion, the coach identifies where there is potential or actual conflict between opposing personality traits. She or he then offers to work through the issue by taking on the role of one half of the pair of opposites. So, for example, she or he might address the issue as the learner's optimistic self, while the learner focuses on how their pessimistic self would react. If required, they can then reverse roles.

Case study   Peter

Peter is an executive director in a public sector agency. A lifelong civil servant until taking on this role, he is a convincing speaker with a good grasp of management jargon and principle. Two years into his current job, it has become clear to his colleagues and the CEO that he has consistently backed away from big decisions that mean dealing with difficult people issues. In particular, he has failed to remove incapable members of his senior team, with the result that key projects are at risk of collapse.

Peter's coach first helped him come to terms with the reality of his situation. To a greater or lesser degree, most of Peter's top team colleagues shared the same behavioural trait, although none so severely as he did. So their frustration had been hidden behind a wall of politeness that had allowed him to convince himself they were supportive and acquiescent. Now, with crisis looming, their feelings were becoming much more difficult to suppress and for Peter to ignore.

The coach steered Peter through a logical discussion of the implications of having not taken key decisions and the likely consequences for himself and the organization if he continued to do so. She also encouraged Peter to talk through his feelings about confronting problem areas and making tough decisions.

Having established that Peter had only two real choices – change his behaviour or find another job – the coach invited him to play out the critical decisions and conversations through personality opposites. First, she invited him to think about situations where he had been 'Mr Nice Guy' and 'Mr Ruthless'. Identifying the latter took some work, but Peter eventually remembered a situation in which he had become so angry at the way he had been treated by a supplier that he had tracked down the company chief executive at home over the weekend and given him a 10-minute dressing down over the telephone.

'How did that feel?'

'Terrifying at the time, but good afterwards. I was really shaking!'

'Did it work?'

'Yes; they were back on site to fix the problem by Monday midday.'

Peter and the coach then went through the conversations he needed to have with his senior team. First they took on the Nice Guy approach, with the coach acting the role of particular team members. Peter was asked to recall how he had felt in previous Nice Guy encounters and how he had opened the discussion. Predictably, the conversation quickly got bogged down and the change objective sidelined.

Then Peter tried the Mr Ruthless approach, which he found difficult. However, he found he could keep the discussion on track and was able to counter excuses forcefully. Combining elements of both Nice Guy and Mr Ruthless – essentially compromising between the two – gave him a template he could feel comfortable with.

Peter had already accepted an offer from the CEO to sit in with him, while he undertook these difficult conversations for real. After the coaching session, he informed the CEO that he would prefer to handle the matter himself – he needed to prove to himself that he could do the task on his own. He rehearsed the most critical conversations with the coach once again, shortly before they happened for real.

Over the subsequent 6 months or so, Peter established the habit of recognizing when tough decisions or conversations were in the offing, and used his coach as a sounding board to prepare for each of them. The defining moment came when he was able to confront the CEO constructively about aspects of *his* behaviour. From this point on, the need for help from the coach diminished rapidly.

Living with roadblocks

Coming to terms with our blocks can need no more than naming and acknowledging them. A powerful and rapid way of doing this is illustrated in Barbara Jakob's *Using intuition to identify roadblocks*.

Using intuition to identify roadblocks
Barbara Jakob

A Mentor/Coach probably wouldn't be a mentor/coach if they hadn't developed their own intuitive dimension or were not an intuitive person anyway by inclination. Meeting the client for the first time involves intuition on both sides. The famous 'first impression' is intuitive and seldom can be explained. Of course, we 'see' the other person's outfit and look on the face which tells us a lot already, but there is often this immediate inner feeling – 'seeing' with the heart. Very often clients come to us in challenging life situations where they are so much burdened that their 'real self' is not obvious anymore. In these situations where we need to build up people, we need our personal intuition to tell us when we reach our limit as a coach and our coachee maybe needs a therapist.

How to help develop intuition?
There is no simple and easy answer to that question. In all coaching and mentoring sessions, asking the appropriate and 'right' questions already has a strong intuitional aspect to it.

Commentary
At the 10th European Mentoring and Coaching Conference, Barbara tried the experiment of asking people to sit in threes and for one person to speak for no more than half a minute. The other two then were invited to guess what the speaker's issue was, and to ask, 'Could it be …?' Those of us in the audience were amazed both at what was said to us – hitting the spot so acutely after such a tiny amount of time – and when we were watching and allowing this intuition to play, how clearly the issues seemed to emerge.

Moving roadblocks

For the active and optimistic helper, this is the part of this chapter that you will naturally be drawn to. That's fine – we are in the business of helping people to change. Nonetheless, the points made at the start of this chapter about exercising wisdom and discretion in deciding what changes to help people make are a reminder of the perspective that suggests that not everything can be changed and not everything that can be changed should be changed.

This warning particularly applies to the fascinating technique outlined by Marilyn Spero, *Mentoring as a double task*. As she herself says, you need psychodynamic understanding and supervision of your practice if you are to work in this way.

Another take on moving roadblocks is the technique *What would an ISTJ say?* This arose from the coincidence of David coaching someone who had the same personal preference type in Myers Briggs terms.

Our final technique for moving roadblocks focuses on the use of time and is called *Capacity management model.*

Mentoring as a double task – addressing task and emotion
Marlene Spero

Managers need adaptability and emotional strength to deal with the tensions and uncertainties found in an increasingly uncertain environment. The best learning occurs when embedded in current work situations.

Today's senior executives face unprecedented challenges. They work in rapidly changing environments, having to deal with increasing complexity and uncertainty. They are less assured of the impact of their decisions or actions than they used to be. They need to be able to use their authority as well as being creative and innovative. Many more demands are placed on them at a personal level. Their capacity to succeed is determined not only by their competencies and capabilities but by their emotions and ability to deal with the tensions and anxieties stirred up by the work. The double task approach to mentoring addresses both individual emotional needs as well as the requirements of work.

The underlying assumptions of this approach are:

(a) Learning can be maximized if it is related to an issue of current concern (the task) as well as reflecting on the 'here and now experience' of the individual (the process).
(b) The work situation, technology, organizational structures, culture, rules, procedures and external processes create tensions that impact on individuals, their beliefs and their ways of thinking and acting and will determine how they manage their role(s) and relationships with others.
(c) The aim of mentoring is to enable individuals to reflect on and make sense of these factors and to reach a new understanding of both the world around them and what is going on inside them, and the interaction between the two.

These ideas, based on psychoanalytical and systemic thinking, are related to the work of Harold Bridger, who coined the term 'double task' (Bridger, 1990). The concept evolved from his work with groups and organizations. The mentoring programme is based on 12 sessions in which continuous process makes it possible to integrate new learning and change. The mentor will attempt to tune in with the individual at both a cognitive and emotional level so as to understand where he is coming from – his early family and life experiences, and his motivation and capacities for the work as well as the context in which he is working and the tasks with which he is confronted. The mentor provides a space in which anxieties and fears can be contained, a place where the mentee can explore his feelings, review what is happening, and reflect on issues of current concern.

The mentor also attempts to bridge the gap between the existing organizational context, culture, values and forms and the new situation, thereby facilitating development and personal change. He reflects, confronts and interprets, using his experience of the mentee's feelings and how he relates to the mentee as a means of furthering the latter's understanding of himself and the world around him. The following examples illustrate this approach.

Case study 1   The HR consultant

The head of HR in a consulting firm and member of a project team of 10 said that he was having difficulties working with his team. He told me that his boss, the founder of the organization who had headed the team, had decided to retire at age 45 to spend more time with his family. The two men had worked closely together and had been involved in some leading-edge projects. He idealized his boss, thought him to be highly creative and said that he had learnt an enormous amount from him. He felt they were particularly creative together – they were seen as the golden boys. He had immediately taken a week's holiday when the boss left and on his return said that he found it impossible to work with the team. He thought it was disintegrating. He said he was very angry and critical of the new manager, a woman who wanted to change the way the team worked.

Although I was aware of his disappointment at not having been invited to be the new team manager, I was more aware of his sadness and feelings of loss of the old boss. The latter had acted as father to him, bringing him along and encouraging him. He now felt very badly let down. I suggested his feelings of anger and sadness were connected with this loss. It was like losing a parent.

He later revealed that his father had died when he was a child and he was brought up in a household of women. This boss had been a replacement father for him. He had not allowed himself to grieve and instead was acting out his anger with his colleagues. Having explored his feelings he was able to re-integrate himself back into the team. We continued to work on developing his role and relationships with his colleagues. The need to understand this father/son relationship, to work through a mourning process, to acknowledge his grief and anger and to face the loss was crucial to his being able to move on and face the reality of his new situation.

Case study 2 The lawyer

A lawyer working in a finance company had been rapidly promoted to head of department. He was younger than many of the lawyers who worked for him and he found it difficult to use his authority and engage with his new role. He did not feel confident in dealing with the Board.

During our numerous conversations, he revealed that he had a father who had bullied and undermined him and it became clear that it was these feelings that were once again evoked whenever he had dealings with the Board. One particular director reminded him of his father. He said he lacked confidence.

He also had difficulties working with a female colleague who he said was not pulling her weight. He felt very aggressive towards her and would overburden her with work. The culture in the organization was sexist and he was aware that he was colluding with it. He said he always found women problematic and would become very authoritarian, aggressive and critical.

As we were talking about this issue he remembered a dream he had had as a child. He had bought his mother some flowers and then remembered walking into a room in which the flowers were strewn all over the floor and feeling very upset and hurt. It was as if mother had destroyed his precious gift. We explored his anxieties and his rage with his mother, which he recognized as mirroring his relationship with his female colleague. Both situations, once explored, became less problematic and his anger diminished. He had been given the space to reflect and to work through some of the emotions that had been aroused in him. He began to feel more confident working with the directors and was able to build a more workable relationship with his female colleague.

Concluding remarks

The above examples are illustrations of the connectedness between emotional issues, the work context and the task. They indicate how the work situation may generate emotional tensions and anxieties within the individual which, once worked through and explored, can be resolved enabling the individual to function in a more integrated and effective way. The transitional space (the ongoing and regular sessions) offered by the mentor helps to facilitate the process of change. Learning is thus maximized by working on the task in hand as well as exploring the here-and-now process as experienced by the individual.

This reflective process is particularly valuable in building self-confidence and competency, and enhancing personal ego strength and insight, as well as furthering an understanding of the individual, his role and the wider organizational context. Working through and understanding emotions and anxieties can deal with many of the problems that get in the way of leadership, for instance, and other capacities can be dealt with. It is these anxieties that inhibit thinking, action and performance.

Anyone adopting this approach would need to have had some personal psychodynamic experience as well as a systemic or socio-technical understanding of organizations. There are training courses available including the Harold Bridger Working Conference, which explores the complexity of individual and organizational life as an ongoing dynamic and reflective process. The Working Conference is run annually by the Bayswater Institute, as is the Professional and Managerial Dilemmas Conference, which is also based on Harold Bridger's design.

Counselling or psychotherapy courses would equip the individual with a psychodynamic understanding of the individual and group processes. An alternative would be to have supervision with an appropriate supervisor, thereby enabling the mentor to explore the mentoring process with the client from both a psychodynamic and organizational perspective as well as the feelings and thoughts evoked in himself. The above are ways of enhancing the mentor's understanding of processes that are 'beneath the surface' in himself, in others and in groups as well as in the organizational context.

What would an ISTJ say?

When you are moving to an action stage in a helping relationship, it is as well to check what the personality type of the two parties is and what their preference is in regard to action. Those familiar with the Myers Briggs Type Inventory may find Hirsh and Kise (2000) useful in seeing characteristic strengths and weaknesses, needs and preferences in the coaching relationship. Another powerful tool for understanding personality is the Enneagram, and for those wishing to have an introduction to its use in coaching, Bast and Thomson (2003), will be helpful.

The case study gives an illustration of an occasion when the two parties were of similar types, but the process of thinking through the implications of type can be just as productive when types are different.

Case study   Two ISTJs

The coach and coachee had an agreeable time exploring possibilities and dreaming up attractive scenarios. They left everything loose at the end and the coachee commented that this was fine as her personality type encouraged this sort of thinking. In Myers Briggs terms she was an ENFP. The coach said that he was an ENFP as well. He then suggested that they play 'What would an ISTJ say now?' This led to an intensive, fun but serious exploration of some hard-edged proposals for checking out the reality, and specifying actions and milestones, review dates and outcomes expected. It added a core of discipline to the relationship, which was becoming comfortable but not challenging. They agreed who would write up notes, and how these would be followed up on the review dates and at subsequent meetings. The two ENFPs agreed (they would, wouldn't they?) that the notes were not there for criticism of the performance of the coachee but to enable the review and understanding of what barriers were arising that stood in the way of making the changes that the coachee wanted.

Capacity management model

The *Capacity management model* is a simple way of helping someone to review how usefully they or their department are using their resources of time, energy, money and materials.

Tasks in quadrant A are enjoyable and fulfilling because they play to the individual or team strengths and they are (or should be) appreciated by others. Tasks in quadrant D are valued by customers and by the organization, but do not play to their current skills and natural talents. As a result, there is typically a tendency to avoid these, or to downgrade them in importance. Quadrant C contains those activities the individual or team is good at (perhaps because they have always done these things, or because that was what the manager did before she or he was promoted). It's very easy to relapse into these in order to avoid thinking about tasks that are genuinely more important. This is classic displacement activity and often accounts for a high level of a person's time at work. Finally, quadrant D consists of activities the person or team is not good at and which are not particularly useful to the customer or the organization. Although there is a natural tendency to avoid these, they have a depressing tendency to appear on people's 'ought to' lists – particularly in appraisals and the personal development plans that derive from them. The problems with focusing on these activities are that:

- there is often no real motivation to tackle them;
- they generate a feeling of guilt that undermines performance in other areas;
- the probability of doing them well is much lower than in any other quadrant, so the impact on personal/functional reputation is negative; and
- they become a continuing distraction from what really matters.

The capacity management model is different from the urgent/important matrix, because it examines both capability and need. A weakness with

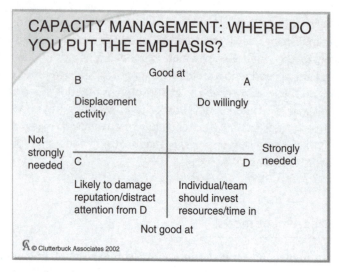

CAPACITY MANAGEMENT: WHERE DO YOU PUT THE EMPHASIS?

© Clutterbuck Associates 2002

Figure 6.2   **Capacity management.**

the urgent/important matrix is that what is important often goes unrecognized because it is too difficult to acknowledge and deal with. To use it properly, you need to have a realistic view of what is and isn't important and where you are capable of making significant improvements and/or doing the task well. It is not much use tackling a task that is important (whether urgent or not), if you do it badly.

Putting the two models together provides a valuable tool for assessing what tasks and responsibilities to let go of and where to concentrate mental energy.

Case study   **Oliver**

Oliver is a senior manager – a regional director – in an insurance company. He has, he says, 'seen so many changes of ownership and structure in the past 10 years that he comes to work each day expecting to do a different job.' He attributes his survival to the fact that he never lost sight of the main goal – to sell high volumes of policies. Even though he is no longer a front-line manager, he still sells a considerable volume himself, or is an active part of teams making pitches at large corporate clients. This, he admits, is where he likes to be and where his natural skills are most effective – closing the sale.

Oliver has been on a variety of leadership programmes – even attending the same one twice, for two different owners of the business – which have emphasized other elements of the senior management role, but he admits that not a lot of the content has stuck. With a new merger looming, he has become aware that his job is on the line. Although he always hits the numbers, he has been informed by HR that good people-development skills will be a key criterion on which decisions will be made about who stays or goes. This was not an area where he had been given very good appraisals in the past. The message was clear – change your style or else.

This was the first time Oliver had worked with a coach and he was very nervous and sceptical. 'I'm not sure I can change the way I am, but I guess your role is to make that happen,' he told her. 'No', she replied. 'My role is to help you work out exactly what you want to change, to help you develop your own plan and support you as best I can in making it happen for yourself.'

It soon became clear to the coach that Oliver had never really analysed his job content, so they agreed she would shadow him for a day. For the week after that, he would also keep a log of what he did, why it was needed and who by. They then sat down together and analysed this data.

What had seemed to Oliver a very clear cut division between the selling role and the people development turned out to be anything but. On the first pass, only about 10 per cent of what he did was genuinely in quadrant A (good at and needed), with the rest spread fairly equally between B (good at and not needed) and D (needed but not good at). Rather than advise him to make a radical shift from C to D, however, the coach explored with Oliver how some of the B activities could be recast to move them into A or D. Oliver was spending a lot of time, for example, overseeing and getting directly involved in preparing bids and contracts – could he adapt the way he tackled this activity, so that instead of fulfilling the role, he was coaching others to do this? Yes, he could.

The coach also encouraged Oliver to gather feedback from his direct reports and peers about what they needed from him, so that he had an even more accurate picture of the capacity management matrix. Analysis of this data revealed a number of activities that clearly belonged in quadrant C (not good at, not needed). The net result was a remarkably swift transformation as Oliver found he enjoyed the challenge of coaching others. He used the coach as a sounding board and observer to increase his skills in the role. After 6 months, they repeated the capacity management analysis and concluded that people development issues had moved from quadrant D to at least the border of quadrant A, if not well inside. They then began to focus on other quadrant D issues.

References

Argyris, C. (1991). Teaching smart people how to learn, *Harvard Business Review*, May–June, 99–109.

Bast, M. and Thomson, C. (2003). *Out of the Box: Coaching with the Enneagram.* Portland, Oregon, Stellar Attractions.

Bridger, H. (1990). Courses and working conferences as transitional learning institutions. In *The Social Engagement of Social Science,* Vol. 1, *The Socio-Psychological Perspective* (Trist, E. and Murray, H., eds). Free Associations Books.

Hirsh, S. A. and Kise, J. A. G. (2000). *Introduction to Type and Coaching.* Palo Alto, CA: Consulting Psychologists Press.

Lee, G. (2003). *Leadership Coaching.* London: CIPD.

Persaud, R. (2001). *Staying Sane: How to Make your Mind Work for You.* London: Bantam.

Chapter 7

Stimulating creative thinking

Why is creative thinking important in personal change?

There are lots of ways of developing creativity and books on how to do it from authors like Buzan (1995) and de Bono (1990) flood the bookshop shelves. In a sense this is odd, because *having* ideas is such a minuscule part of making change happen. Having the idea can get you on a path but there is still an awful-long way to go before the new idea is learned and internalized as a habit, before other people are persuaded, and aspects of the organization changed so as to let the new idea live. However, in the context of coaching and mentoring, thinking creatively is important, because our habitual responses lock us into patterns of behaviour that are often self-defeating and do not deliver what it is that we are intending. Chapters 2–5 have a number of techniques for being creative around clarifying what the problem is. Chapter 6 – *Dealing with Roadblocks* – was about the demolition of some of these barriers and this chapter is about finding what to put in the place of the block. Chapters 8 and 9 include some approaches to creative solutions. This chapter focuses upon creativity – how to do things rather than what to do.

One of our colleagues in training senior mentors, Peter English, runs a session on *Being live*. He introduces ideas of noticing one's own feelings in the conversation and being open and exploratory about them, and also doing the same for the mentee's feelings. Another angle on being live is to notice language used, and the first activity in this chapter pays particular attention to how to respond to *clichés*. McLeod (2003) is a good source for other techniques picking up language and he highlights a string of 'linguistic tips' throughout the book. We also include a version of a helpful technique to deal with *Competing Commitments*, from Mike Turner, which originally appeared in his newsletter (www.mikethementor.co.uk).

Richard Hale's *Identifying values and belief in learning relationships* is a rich multi-stage technique, and his *Throwing away a role* activity within it was one of the favourites for one of us in studying the techniques we were sent by our co-authors. Kate Hopkinson offers a range of activities for opening up people's perception of their problems, and Vivien Whitaker gives an example of how she works with Russian dolls or other objects to model the helpee's perception of team dynamics. We conclude with a short think piece about being lucky. Is it the helper's role to encourage the helpee to think lucky?

Clichés

There is only one situation less creative than being a learner who speaks in clichés all the time, and that is having both helper and learner speaking in clichés.

Case study   **James mentors Kevin**

On one occasion when we were watching a pair of chief executives co-mentoring, we witnessed the following exchange:

Kevin: Poor performance is tolerable in the first year as a new director, but it is not acceptable in the second year. The right words are coming out, but the actions don't match.

James: And actions speak louder than words, at the end of the day.

Now Kevin may not have been especially live, as he was trotting out arbitrary rules or dicta for judging executive performance, but the situation is made much worse by James reinforcing the unconsidered nature of the discourse by using a striking double cliché.

On this occasion the interaction continued for a while and the observer then intervened and explored what else James might have done to bring more life into the discussion. Suggestions included:

* asking how actions and words didn't match;
* asking what prevented the actions not matching;
* asking how Kevin felt about the director's continuing under-performance;
* asking about the rule that under-performance is OK in the first year, but not in the second; does it always make sense to be tolerant at the start and then intolerant?

All these avenues bring a concrete questioning approach into the conversation and enable creative problem solving to begin. Hector Berlioz famously said:

Time is a great teacher; it's a shame it kills all its pupils.

As coaches and mentors we need this irreverent attitude to clichés.

Competing commitments
Mike Turner

How is it that, despite being committed to change, we so often fail to make changes we are committed to? If we are not making happen what we claim to be committed to, then there must be a stronger, competing commitment to which we are unknowingly committed.

The process for uncovering this stronger competing commitment is simple and effective and can be used with both individuals and groups.

1. *Commitment*: Identify something that is important to you to have or that you value which you don't yet have in your life. Make this commitment explicit by completing the stem: '**I am committed to ...**'
2. *Behaviour*: Given that the commitment you have just identified is not being fulfilled in your life, complete the stem: '**What I'm doing, or not doing, that is preventing my commitment being fully realized, is ...**'
3. *Competing Commitment*: Given what you're doing, or not doing, what does this suggest you're actually committed to? That is, identify the stronger more compelling outcome that you are actually committed to (the competing commitment). Complete the stem: '**I may also be committed to ...**'
4. *Big Assumption*: Driving your competing commitment will be an assumption that you treat as true. To uncover this Big Assumption, complete the stem: '**I assume that if my competing commitment is (not) met, ...**' with how you might feel then. (If you come up with something that unnerves you a little, then you are probably on track. If you come up with something noble, you probably need to try again!)

For example:

- *Commitment*: **I am committed to** managing my time better and having a better work-life balance.
- *Behaviour*: **What I'm doing that prevents my commitment from being more fully realized is** working weekends, over-preparing and procrastinating.
- *Competing Commitment*: '**I may also be committed to** doing perfect work.'
- *Big Assumption*: '**I assume that if** I'm not perfect, I'll be rejected.'

If we then read this sequence backwards, we can see that, given the Big Assumption, it is entirely appropriate to pursue the competing commitment and, in turn, to behave in a way that prevents us achieving our actual goal.

Sometimes, merely being aware of the conflicting commitments allows us to change our behaviour. If not, one way forward is to find ways to challenge the Big Assumption that drives the dynamic. For example:

- noticing evidence that challenges it (when I screw up I actually don't get thrown out);
- exploring its origins, and whether it is still relevant (I've been sent away to school because I'm not working hard enough); or
- finding opportunities to test it and see how we feel (do a good enough rather than a perfect piece of work).

As we recognize that the Big Assumption is not the truth, so we free ourselves to achieve our commitments.

Identifying values and belief in learning relationships
Richard Hale, Value Projects Ltd (www.viprojects.com)

An important factor in determining whether a learning relationship will succeed concerns the issue of personal values and beliefs. My research has shown that where learning relationships have broken down it is often due to the insensitivity of one or both of the parties to the differences that may exist in terms of personal values and beliefs.

It is not that values and beliefs have to be same, though it is possible that some may be so opposed that it does make the relationship untenable. It is more of an issue related to the human condition whereby we tend to look at the world and other people, starting with our own perspective. So the danger is in assuming others have, or should have, values and beliefs similar to our own.

Recognizing and accepting differences is more likely to lead to a sustainable relationship than assuming the other person should have the same values as yourself or seeking to impose your values on others.

It is thought that each of us is motivated by a small number of core values which drive us in all that we do, whether in work or outside. So, for example, core values might influence choice of career, friends and lifestyle.

These are different to the behaviours and skills that we display; they are deeper.

Shown below are just five examples of values and beliefs with descriptors:

Equality	I feel strongly about equality of opportunity in terms of, for instance, age, gender, and background
Respect for Authority	It is important to respect authority and in most cases to defer to those in a more senior position

Independence	It is essential that I retain independence and choice in most things I do
Inner Sense of Control	I am driven by a sense that I can influence events and my own destiny
Conformity	I believe in conforming to the rules and system in most cases

These are drawn from a profile of 30 values and beliefs and part of a values diagnostic available from www.viprojects.com. However, you may wish initially to explore this subject by using the short exercises shown below. These can be completed in the mentoring/coaching pair in order to open up the discussion about how your values and beliefs compare.

Having worked on the identification of the beliefs and values it is interesting to ask yourself the tough personal question:

Is this how I really am and do these values and beliefs influence my actions and behaviour?

or

Is this more about how I would like to be or see myself and do my behaviours and actions actually say something else?

Be aware though that this is a very personal subject and some people will not want to share such issues with others. Some have even described how delving into such issues raises difficult questions at a personal level. However, this should not be an excuse for ignoring the subject. In coaching and mentoring relationships the more that can be done to clarify matters and be open and sensitive to values and beliefs early in the relationship, the better.

Values and beliefs exercise

1. *Personal credo*
   Draft a personal motto that describes how you try to live your life
   Example – Winners never quit, quitters never win
   alternatively,
   What would you like to have on a family coat of arms?
   Example – From thorns come grapes
2. *The epitaph/memorial/leaving speech*
   Write your obituary using no more than 100 words to describe your life and achievements. Alternatively, using no more than 25 words, consider what you would like to have as an epitaph. If that seems too depressing then maybe write your own leaving speech which you

would like to hear if you were to leave your current organization or retire.

3. *Throw away a role*

   Imagine the roles that you play in your life and write these down on different pieces of paper, i.e. husband/wife, manager/director, member of sports club. Now select a role that is least important to you and 'throw it away'!

   Reflect on how your life would be if you did not have this role any more. What was important about this role?

   Repeat this process until you have thrown all the roles away

It is important to respect the privacy of others who may not be keen to disclose or explore personal values publicly. People may find it easier to discuss their personal skills or behaviours rather than their values and beliefs. So this is a practical way into the discussion about values, starting with behaviours and then asking how these behaviours may be manifestations of certain personal beliefs.

When you can encourage open discussion, disclosure and comparison between your own and another's beliefs and values, the rewards will be plain to see. The level at which people begin to understand one another deepens and often people will describe uncovering things about themselves they had not previously known about.

Helping people articulate complex problems
Kate Hopkinson

A useful principle here is to encourage coachees to start *somewhere*, and then meander in whatever direction makes sense to them:

(i) Where and how they meander is information in itself
(ii) It is quicker to get *something* out, however confused, which you can subsequently work on, than force them to try to be very logical about it (a move which may also undermine rapport, since they may read it as critical of them).

Once you've got a 'draft version,' you can utilize any or all of the following to help you to see the connections and understand the ramifications:

● Spidergrams – Mind Maps (Buzan, 1995) can be very helpful in teasing out connections in a complex situation or issue.
● Other forms of drawing, for example:
  – *Time Lines*: Use a horizontal axis as development over time. A refinement here is to draw a horizontal line, and invite the coachee

to place positive aspects of the situation above the line, and negative ones below it, moving through time from left to right.

- *Archery target*: Put the coachee in the bull's eye, and then place other people closer or further away (using concentric circles as demarcations). Describe who they are, and what their part in the situation is. Refinement: have a 'pie slice' of the circle (or even a semi-circle) represent a particular salient group – e.g. enemies.

This technique is particularly useful where you have a 'cast of thousands'

1. Story perspectives: ask the coachee to run through the story several times, as seen from different people's perspectives (e.g. themselves, their boss, an outsider).
2. Ask for a 'headline' describing the nub of the issue. Then ask for examples of the headline, from the situation.
3. Invite the coachee to liken the situation to several different analogies ('It's like a bear pit in there'; 'it's like living in a Force 10 gale'; 'It's like nuclear winter'). Then ask them how (a) it is *like* each analogy; and (b) how it is *unlike* each analogy.
4. Introduce them to the distinction between the 'truth of the physical world,' and the 'truth of human being.' In the former, things cannot be both something and its opposite at the same time. So a crow cannot be both black and not black. On the other hand, social truth can and does encompass paradox. Something can be frightening and enjoyable at the same time. A person can be both helpful and unhelpful at the same time. In other words, legitimize (apparent) contradictions as reasonable and, quite possibly, true. This will give a much richer picture of their perceptions when they don't feel that they have to iron them into a logically coherent narrative.

Analysis using modelling
Vivien Whitaker

The process of modelling involves using objects, e.g. pebbles, plastic cups or Russian dolls, to set out or model a situation.

It can be helpful in the context of a mentoring or coaching discussion as it:

- provides a snapshot summary of a complex situation
- assists the mentee or coachee to see a situation that they are involved in from a distance, which can assist their objectivity
- offers variety for the activist, kinaesthetic mentee or coachee who finds discussion rather abstract
- encourages an exploration of how a situation is at present

● stimulates the coachee or mentee to speculate about how they would like the situation to be in the future.

Russian dolls, which stack one inside the other, have certain advantages over the use of pebbles or paper cups, as it is possible to vary size according to how powerful each of the people seems in relation to one another. The distance between the dolls/cups/stones indicates the strength of relationships within the situation – the shorter the distance, the stronger the link.

After a model of the present dynamics of a situation has been developed, the next challenge is to work out how the mentee or coachee would like things to be in the future.

Case study   **Barbara**

Barbara has just become a team leader. She has requested the assistance of a mentor to help her develop her leadership style and explore her relationship with her new team.

She recognizes that she is a 'hands-on' kind of person so has chosen to use the Russian dolls to analyse how her new team is functioning at present.

Initially she identifies the informal groupings within the team, identifying those members who have social power (though not necessarily status or position power). She decides that the size of the dolls she is using is linked to informal influence rather than role.

She positions those who work closely together near to each other and explains the relationships between sub-groupings as she moves the dolls around.

When she has modelled the current team dynamics to her satisfaction, including herself within the model, her mentor asks probing questions about the dynamics of the relationships.

Then the mentor asks Barbara to change the model to how Barbara would like the team to function in the future, changing both distances between the dolls and the sizes of the dolls, if appropriate.

Once the future model has been developed, discussion focuses on action planning and the necessary practical steps needed to bring about the changes.

Lucky

Do the people you help think that they are lucky in life or unlucky? It seems to matter what they think (Persaud, 2001, pp. 401–5). People who said that they were unlucky, when given a task to complete in one minute by a psychologist, typically gave up within 30 seconds.

The lucky ones went beyond the time limit and said things like, 'No, hang on; I'm nearly there.' So, belief in your luck links with being perserverant – an important predictor of success in many complex tasks.

These experimental subjects were also given a newspaper and asked to count the number of pictures in it. Those reporting themselves as unlucky went through to the end and said '52,' or some such. The lucky ones however, often noticed a half-page statement in the middle of the paper saying, 'If you stop now and point this out to the psychologist, he will give you a big prize.' None of the unluckies spotted this but three quarters of the luckies did. An interesting parable. Does it mean that if a coachee told us something that they were not good at and so were invited to imagine that they were good at it, then this might make a difference to their performance? Some NLP trainers think that it would (McDermott and Jago, 2001, pp. 94–6). And Albert Einstein famously said that the most important question to ask is 'Do you think that the universe is benign?'

Exercise – Are you feeling lucky?

Clint Eastwood has given the question 'Are you feeling lucky?' a whole new meaning, but we find that there are times when exploring the concept of luck can help people make better decisions. A common example is when people compare themselves against someone more successful, in their perception.

'How did they get on so well?'
'I'm sure there was a strong element of luck in it'
'What do you think they did to make themselves lucky?'

A set of questions we have used to good effect is the following:

- How much do you think the outcome depends on luck here?
- How lucky do you feel compared to the other players?
- To what extent do you think feeling unlucky is affecting how you approach this issue (e.g. your confidence levels)?
- Would you behave differently if you felt lucky?
- What's the difference between the luckiest players and you?
- What could you do to make yourself luckier?
- What, if any, are the down-sides of playing and not winning?
- How will you feel, if you do win?

The realization that even pessimists can make their own luck often initiates a discussion about how much the individual wants to achieve a goal and how they can increase the chances of a lucky break occurring.

References

Buzan, T. (1995). *Use Your Head*. London: BBC Books.

De Bono, E. (1990). *Six Thinking Hats*. Harmondsworth: Penguin.

McDermott, I. and Jago, W. (2001). *The NLP Coach*. London: Piatkus.

McLeod, A. (2003). *Performance Coaching: The Handbook for Managers, H. R. Professionals and Coaches*. Bancyfelin, Carmarthen: Crown House.

Persaud, R. (2001). *Staying Sane: How to Make Your Mind Work for You*. London: Bantam.

Chapter 8

Deciding what to do

Introduction

Perhaps one of the chief reasons people take on a coach or mentor is for help in the subject area of this chapter – deciding what to do. Sensing that one is at a crossroads or a roundabout can lead individuals to seek help in choosing the right road ahead. Being on the horns of a dilemma is painful and deciding one way or the other can be a relief. The people we are helping may be faced with too few choices or too many. Sometimes we need to help them think about other options in order to loosen the tyranny of the current situation. On other occasions, they may be paralysed by too much choice, and we need to find ways of helping them to focus down on one path. Acting or not acting is another way the decision can be presented, and it is well to remember that there are times when, paradoxically, the status quo is the way forward.

It is said that there are four things we can do if we are in a situation where we are dissatisfied:

● Change the situation
● Move out of the situation
● Change ourselves
● Put up with the situation.

Our helping can focus on any of these. In fact offering the person we are helping the four options is useful in focusing their minds.

In this chapter, following Samuel Johnson's dictum, we have emphasized techniques that focus upon learners deciding to change themselves. They progress from techniques to help with doing less to techniques to get us to move into action. *Busy fool syndrome* and *maximizer/minimizer* suggests a way of working towards doing less rather than more. *Consequences* encourages us to pay attention to what will happen if we don't make the decision as well as what will happen if we do. *General to specific* proposes that sometimes the learner will not act because they have not narrowed things down to what the issue is that they wish to address. *Hierarchy of needs* offers a means of being clear about our motives in moving forward. *Setting the direction* helps the learner to manage the process of moving to action, as does Vivien Whitaker's technique *Using the metaphor of a roundabout. Appreciative inquiry* represents the end of the spectrum focused upon energizing and vitalizing action.

Changing ourselves

Busy fool syndrome

Heike Bruch and Sumantra Ghoshal claim in a challenging *Harvard Business Review* article (Bruch and Ghoshal, 2002), that 90 per cent of managers lack the core combination of high focus and high energy that makes for genuine effectiveness. Here are some ways to help managers recognize that they have a problem.

Whose jobs are you doing, in addition to your own?
The coach/mentor discusses with the learner what the elements of their role are that:

(a) have greatest potential to add value;
(b) enable direct reports to achieve more;
(c) deliver longer-term, sustainable benefits.

The question, *Why do you have to do this?*, occurs frequently. Other questions include:

- Would the team achieve more if you were able to focus on more strategic issues, or simply spend more time reflecting on what it does and how?
- How much of your time do you spend doing jobs that would be better done by people who report to you?
- What tasks do you do because you enjoy them, rather than because they are important?
- What important issues or tasks have you put off dealing with this week?
- What mechanism do you have for getting to grips with such issues?
- What important issues or tasks have you prevented someone else from resolving recently?

Maximizer or minimizer?

This approach can be helpful in dealing with 'paralysis by analysis'. Recent research divides people into two personality types: maximizers and minimizers. When you are faced with wide choices, do you:

- Cut to the quick and identify 'good enough' solutions?
- Agonize over the 'best solution'?

If you are more like the first, you are a maximizer; if more like the second, a minimizer. Minimizers get more done and their mistakes are sometimes more rapidly obvious. Minimizers can be seen as procrastinators and tend to have much higher levels of stress. Part of the problem for maximizers is that they are so aware of the nuances of performance they are looking for that any minor failing becomes exaggerated. If they buy consumer goods, they will continue to make comparisons after the purchase. As new and better versions come to market, they feel increasingly less satisfied with what they have.

Having too much choice or too little choice are both disempowering. In the work context, the inability to manage choice inhibits decision-making and increases the anxiety that comes from uncertainty. A set of questions we have used successfully to help people manage choice is in Table 8.1.

Also helpful for managing the discussion is the matrix in Figure 8.1.

Table 8.1   Context and process questions in making choices

Context questions	Process questions
• Why do you have to make a choice? (What are the consequences of not doing so?) • Who else can/should you be sharing this decision with? • How quickly is the situation likely to change after the decision is made? • What's the down-side of getting it totally wrong? Partially wrong? • How easily will you be able to forgive yourself if you make a less than perfect choice? A wrong choice?	• How much choice do you *need* to feel comfortable about this decision? • How many criteria do you have? • How can you reduce these criteria to a maximum of three? • How many choices meet these three criteria? • Does one choice stand out as clearly the overall best based on these three criteria? If not, what other criteria can you add that would differentiate between the choices? • Can you increase the flexibility of your choice (i.e. build in the potential for change with changing circumstances)?

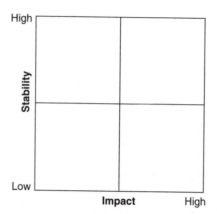

Figure 8.1   Stability vs. impact of choices.

What will happen ...	What will happen if I do it:	What will happen if I don't do it:
	What will not happen if I do it:	What will not happen if I don't do it:
What will not happen ...	... if I do it	... if I don't do it

Figure 8.2   Consequences matrix.

The stability of the decision refers to how long circumstances will remain the same, or sufficiently similar not to bring into question the decision criteria. Impact refers to how serious the consequences are of getting it wrong. Designing a space shuttle or an oil refinery would provide lots of situations for high-stability, high-impact decisions, where it pays to spend a lot of time thinking through and making sure the right choices are made. But selecting between candidates for regional sales manager, in a volatile trading business, might be a high-impact, low-stability decision. Understanding the context typically leads to better and more appropriate processes that break through the excess of choice.

Consequences

When a coachee–mentee is considering a course of action the matrix given in Figure 8.1 can be used to help them look at all the consequences of doing or not doing the thing that is being considered. The particular feature of this matrix that adds to its discriminatory power is that it includes consideration of what will not happen as well as what will happen.

Case study   Mark's move

Mark, a senior manager in the European HQ of a US-based global company, was considering whether to take a promotion that would involve living in the USA. One of the key insights he gained from this framework was thinking through what would not happen if he took it. He recognized that his opportunities for quality time with his growing family and also holiday time to pursue a passionately held hobby of seeking out rare butterflies would be curtailed given the US attitude to holidays in contrast with the European style. He ultimately decided not to go.

Case study   David's PhD

In another example, one of the authors was struggling to complete his PhD thesis while also doing a demanding fulltime job (in fact both of us have had this struggle, but this is the story of just one of us). His mentor got him to focus particularly upon the consequences of not completing the process. The vivid picture that was evoked was just too painful to imagine, and the negative consequences were sufficiently persuasive to lead to a final push that led to the eventual successful completion of the thesis. Looking back, the mentee was clear that it was this conversation that represented the turning point that led to a successful outcome.

Activity

Consider a decision that you are pondering about and with your partner. Complete all four boxes on the matrix. Make the consequences of each as vivid to you as you can. Have you added new perspectives as a result? What direction does this lead you to adopt?

Hierarchy of needs

Maslow's hierarchy of needs (Maslow, 1954) has been one of the staples of management education for 50 years, though Maslow's writing is often little understood (Watson, 1996). The hierarchy remains a somewhat abstract concept for many people. A simple adaptation and personalization of the approach can often provide acute personal insight. The questioning process runs along the following lines:

> *Imagine you were shipwrecked. Once you had food and shelter, what would your first, second and third priorities be?*
>
> *Imagine you suddenly lost your job through disability (your own or needing to devote your time to a sick family member). What would your first, second and third priorities be?*

Bringing the issue closer to the present reality:

What would you miss most about having to give up what you do? (This gives an insight into what the person values about their job.)

- *What inner drives does each of these things address?*
- *Which inner needs do you feel are most fully/least fully satisfied from your work?*
- *What compensation strategies do you use to bridge the gap?*
- *In what other ways might you address those needs? (What other strategies could you adopt?)*

Based on these data, it will normally be possible to draw an individualized hierarchy of needs.

Maslow's contention was that people need to satisfy the lowest levels of need before they can progress to the higher. It is, clearly, difficult to focus on self-actualization if you are starving! But these customized hierarchies tend to allow for a degree of partial satisfaction at most or all levels.

Useful questions here include:

- What do you think this hierarchy says about you?
- Are other people aware of your personal hierarchy of need?
- How well does this fit with what they need from you, or what the organization needs from you?
- What does this tell you about the kind of job/lifestyle that would suit you best?

You can ask the person you are helping, to re-draw their own hierarchy presented as a triangle with chunks of each layer bitten away depending on the extent to which that need has already been met. This opens the way for a discussion of how the under-met needs might be tackled. Useful questions include:

- *What prevents you from feeling fulfilled in each of these areas?*
- *What could you do differently to meet each of these needs?*

- *Do some of these needs conflict? Is it possible to make them mutually supportive?*
- *What compromises do you make now?*
- *What different compromises would you be willing to make? Would you achieve a better overall picture if you did?*

Setting the direction

When we are working with a mentee, we often follow the line of their interest, and the conversation develops from what they say, combined with an element of influence from the particular aspects of their comments that we pick up on.

Make a note of the questions you ask in a mentoring session and, briefly, the responses of your mentee. After 10 minutes or so, suggest to the mentee that you stop and review where the conversation has gone and where it could most usefully go for them next.

Pursue this direction, then stop after another 10 minutes and check again. The mentee may want to continue and perhaps deepen the direction that you have taken, or it may be time to branch out again. Get into the habit of introducing this option as a regular part of letting your mentee determine the direction of the conversation.

Remember, questions, particularly probing questions, do not leave the mentee wholly in command. In fact, if over-used they can become like an interrogation.

Case study   **Carmel grills Jean**

Carmel, an incisive accountant, was coaching Jean, who was her junior. In attempting to support Jean and not to put her own ideas into the equation, Carmel asked a string of open questions. But that was all she did. In reviewing the session Jean confessed that the experience was a bit like being grilled by a suspicious Inland Revenue inspector. Good training perhaps, but not what she expected from a coaching session. Carmel asked whether it would have been better if she had made more suggestions. Jean said not; rather, what she would have liked was a sense that she knew where the conversation was going. Carmel's supervisor used the *Setting the direction* technique and Carmel recognized that this was what Jean needed in their next session.

Using the metaphor of a roundabout
Vivien Whitaker

Our future is not a puzzle to which there is one right answer. Development involves looking at all possible options and choosing the most appropriate one.

The process of using metaphor involves us in comparison of one thing in terms of another. The insights we get from this pairing can help us develop our ideas. The metaphor many people talk about in terms of their career is about being at a crossroads. We find this metaphor limiting as it only offers four possible options. We have found that the metaphor of a roundabout offers many more possibilities and provides more scope for the imagination.

This kinaesthetic activity engages the right side of the brain and can produce insights that may not occur through auditory conversation, using the left logical side of the brain.

Process

Using a sheet of flipchart paper and large pens, encourage your coachee or mentee through the following steps:

1. Ask them to imagine standing at a roundabout. Get them to draw the number of possible exits (opportunities) that they consider are available to them at the moment – even the most unlikely.
   - There may be a road linked to what they wanted to do when young but their parents/carers thought this was impractical or impossible because of lack of funds or lack of 'suitability.'
   - There may be a road linked to recurring dreams or fantasies.
   - There may be a road that involves them in more risk or unknown factors than they face at present.
   - There may be a well defined road which they have been on for some time which feels as 'comfy as an old pair of slippers'.
   - There may be a road that their intuition is urging them to follow, but which other people say is not in their interests.
2. Explore each possible road/exit in turn in discussion together. Metaphorically walk up each road and identify the possibilities of this route forward. Reassure your mentee or coachee that they do not need to move forward on any of the routes. It is sufficient at present to recognize that they have alternatives open to them.
3. Get them to note down the positives and negatives of each potential route.
4. Ask your mentee or coachee for their gut reaction to each route – a route may feel safe or sensible but does it feel exciting? What stirs their energy?
5. Now get them to put a large cross at the beginning of all the roads they don't want to go down.
6. When they are left with two or more routes, develop the appropriate number of different possible future scenarios and encourage your mentee or coachee to research each of them further.

7. Suggest that your mentee or coachee takes their flipchart drawing of their roundabout and put it in a place where they can look at it frequently. Encourage them to share with their partner or family, if appropriate, to gain their reactions and feedback.

Case studies

One person followed this process and developed his roundabout to his satisfaction. When he and his mentor were reviewing the routes they realized that he hadn't included his present job within the roundabout at all. This was a strong indicator about how the mentee was feeling about his present post and provided an impetus to assist him to move on.

Another coachee developed the metaphor further by identifying her motorways, major roads and minor roads in different colours and widths. Some of her roads were straight, some twisting and some had junctions.

After completing this exercise, many people felt excited by the range of options open to them.

Appreciative inquiry

AI, or Appreciative Inquiry (Srivastva and Cooperrider, 1990), is primarily an organizational development, whole systems changing methodology. However, it seems to us to have some intriguing possibilities for coaching.

The start of the AI process is the Affirmative Topic Choice. AI advocates say that the seeds of change are implicit in the very first questions we ask. (This throws an interesting light on the opening, 'Would you tell me a bit about yourself?' Does this question tend to imply there is a fixed self, not amenable to change and development?) For AI the first question tends to be something like, 'What do you want to learn about and achieve?' This is followed by questions checking whether the first response is all that is wanted, until the respondent gets to the point of being emphatically clear about what they really want. This gives a focus for what follows.

At the heart of AI is the appreciative interview. The interview is about discovering information based on the questions 'What gives life to your being in the organization?'; 'What is the best there is here?'; 'What do you most appreciate about your work here?' Could this be the basis for our coaching conversations? Can we see life in the organization not as a problem to be analysed, planned for and solved, but rather as an appreciation and valuing of what is best, an envisioning of what might be and a dialogue with others affected about what should be? This latter approach experiences life in the organization as a mystery to be embraced. The aim is to find the 'positive change core'. This can be seen in coaching as the essence of every strength, innovation, achievement, imaginative story, hope, positive tradition, passion and dream that the individual has, engaged in the pursuit of the Affirmative Topic.

The four-stage AI process (the 4Ds) is:

1. Discovery – mobilize a systemic inquiry into the positive change core.
2. Dream – envision the individual's greatest potential for positive influence and impact on the world.
3. Design – craft a way of going on in which the positive change core is boldly alive in all strategies, processes, systems, decisions and collaborations.
4. Destiny – invite action inspired by the discovery, dream and design.

This framework can represent a process for developing a coaching relationship over time.

References

Bruch, B. and Ghoshal, S. (2002). Beware the busy manager. *Harvard Business Review*, **80**(2), 62–9.

Maslow, A. (1954). *Motivation and Personality*. New York: Harper & Row.

Srivastva, S. and Cooperrider, D. L. (eds) (1990). *Appreciative Management and Leadership: The Power of Positive Thought and Action in Organizations*. San Francisco: Jossey-Bass.

Watson, T. (1996). 'Motivation: that's Maslow, isn't it?' *Management Learning*, **27**(4), 447–64.

Chapter 9

Committing to action

Introduction

One of the principal contributions that coaching and mentoring can make is in helping people commit to action. W H Murray, the pioneer Scottish climber from before and after the Second World War, said (Murray, 2002, p. 279):

> Until one is committed there is hesitancy, the chance to draw back, always ineffectiveness. Concerning all acts of initiative and creation, there is one elementary truth, ignorance of which kills countless ideas and splendid plans: that the moment one commits oneself, then providence moves too. All kind of things occur to help one that would not otherwise have occurred. ... I have a deep respect for one of Goethe's couplets:
>
>> Whatever you can do, or dream you can, begin it,
>> Boldness has genius, power, and magic in it.

Coaches and mentors can help with this process of commitment. One way we do this is to check out where the reservations are (see Chapter 6) and then let the individual's energy move them into action. The technique *Head, heart, guts,* addresses this dynamic. Another approach to dealing with reservations is to focus upon the emotions involved in setting goals. Phil Donnison's description of *The role of emotions in coaching* is useful here – it looks at models that show how a coach can help people make positive use of their emotions during a coaching relationship. Yet another technique is to use Gillian Hill's powerful framework for *Challenging deeply held beliefs and assumptions*. Perhaps the classic model for working on commitment is calibrating it on a 10-point scale – see for example Whitmore (2003). Our example of this technique is called *The meaning of 'yes'*. One feature that stops people committing is a perception of danger in taking action. Sometimes it pays to more closely examine the dragons we perceive to be lurking and we have a technique for this called *Danger? What's dangerous about that?*

The use of personal development planning in coaching and mentoring is well established. Megginson and Whitaker (2003) offer a huge range of techniques, which are not repeated here; however, Linda Phipps describes vividly her useful method of *Personal skills development planning* in this chapter; then there is the case of Craig, *Planning is not enough*.

One of the dynamics that coaches and mentors find themselves dealing with on a regular basis is the paradox of persistence and flexibility. On the one hand we want to encourage our learners to be persistent because that yields results (Persaud, 2001, p. 435). On the other hand, knowing when to give up and letting go of excess baggage are also a part of effectiveness (Megginson and Whitaker, 2003, pp. 105–7). We don't offer a technique for this – we just offer these references and encourage you to be aware of the paradox.

Check out the reservations

Head, heart and guts

Whenever we consider a course of action we can engage thinking, feeling and willing – head, heart and guts. It may be that these different faculties give us different answers, and the unacknowledged war between them can fill us with anxiety and impede our taking action.

This technique suggests that you ask the person you are helping to see what message they are getting from these three aspects of themselves. As they speak, it is useful to note non-verbal cues and to feed these back: 'I noticed that you were talking quietly when you were saying what your feelings were. What might that be about?' or 'Your face lit up when you were describing what your will told you'.

Having explored all three aspects of their perception of the choice, the next step is to explore contradictions or alternatives. Is there a way of treating the alternatives as 'both… and…' options rather than 'either… or…'? If there isn't, where is the energy? Where does the mentee–coachee feel the stronger impulse to act? What can be done about the inhibiting forces?

Case study

Kimberley was a lawyer who was considering giving up her profitable practice, where she worked part-time while contributing, with her husband, to child care. She wanted to move into full-time work as a professional coach. Somehow she was finding it difficult to make the first step. When working through the 'head, heart, guts' technique, she came to the following views:

Head: More possibilities; concerned whether I am making myself too woolly; not yet got strong enough data to know whether I can make a go of it.

Heart: Drawn to working with bigger companies; but these will be a greater challenge to get into.

Guts: I have got to tackle my lack of confidence that I can make it in an unfamiliar area where I do not have years of experience.

The part of this story that came through most powerfully was the issue of confidence. This was interesting, because Kimberley, like many lawyers, prepared meticulously for her session and the lengthy paper outlining advantages and disadvantages did not mention or hint at matters of self-confidence. In the session, she explored this some more. She talked about how her confidence as a young woman in her academic and professional success had been worn down by a series of setbacks through more recent years. She said that it was her determination that had pulled her through the setbacks. She also noticed that if she followed her gut feeling of lack of confidence, it would be self-defeating, because she could not have enough information about how she might fare in her chosen field unless she had a go. She determined to push ahead with building the new business and to work on confidence by noticing occasions when she was more confident than usual and exploring what it was about these situations that made this possible. This would provide an indication of where and how she might work in building the new stream of work.

The role of emotions in coaching
Phil Donnison

This approach to coaching acknowledges the role that emotions play in the coaching process. It is based on research that identifies how a person's perception of a situation can have a beneficial or detrimental effect on his/her performance. Three theoretical descriptions are selected which seek to explain how emotions can help or hinder progress towards the sort of outcomes typically sought from coaching.

1. The Yerkes-Dodson Law (1908) identifies how the level at which an individual performs in a given task can be undermined if they find the task too challenging, or if they do not find it challenging enough.
2. Vince and Martin (1993) describe how an individual's feelings and emotions can serve to encourage or discourage activities towards learning and development.
3. In my own research (Donnison, 2000) I found that people need a specific climate to be able to learn from mistakes and failures as well as from success and accomplishments.

The theoretical explanations provided from these sources serve as a basis for an approach to coaching which ensures that emotions are used to support the outcomes of the coaching process.

A person involved in a coaching process often sets a plan of action that helps them to carry out their intentions. They may plan to practise new skills, develop new ways of thinking or use new techniques. However, all plans carry a degree of risk of failure, and anxiety about the possibility of failure can hinder performance. For instance, someone feeling anxious about a test or exam often finds that worrying too much gets in the way. Their fear of failure becomes a self-fulfilling prophecy.

As a result, individuals may start to take no risks at all, stick with what they know and avoid anything that is not tried and tested. The Yerkes-Dodson Law seeks to explain how, if risks are completely avoided, individuals can become bored and stale, and improvements in performance can become unlikely as the individual is very anxious. The curvilinear relationship between anxiety and performance suggests that improved performance is most likely when individuals perceive that an activity carries a moderate level of risk. This suggests that coaches should encourage individuals to set goals which stand a reasonable chance of success, rather than egging them on towards over-ambitious targets or letting them off the hook with plans that easily can be achieved. If this is the case, how can a coach encourage a person to commit to actions that the latter sees as carrying a moderate risk?

If a person feels that they are committing themselves to too great a risk, anxiety can lead to fight or flight, defensiveness or avoidance, all of which will hamper performance improvement. Vince and Martin point to a cycle of action learning that can promote learning, in which individuals are able to live with the difficult emotions evoked by feeling at risk. They suggest that if individuals can hold on to their anxiety, contain their fears and live with the uncertainty of unknown situations, they are more likely to gain new insights and develop new capabilities.

How can coaches support people who are feeling these 'difficult' emotions? My own research suggests people can learn from failure and mistakes if they are able to manage, or even by-pass, feelings which are associated with the possibility of failure and negative outcomes, feelings such as disappointment, inadequacy or vulnerability. The climate for learning that makes this possible sustains people who are taking risks, encourages emotions that support learning and facilitates learning and development regardless of task outcomes.

This suggests that, to take full advantage of coaching, people require a climate with several key features:

1. The understanding that the coach's purpose is to release potential, not correct deficiencies.
2. Support and encouragement from the coaching and anyone who is associated with the coaching process.
3. A willingness to talk openly about any aspects of their plan that cause them to feel inadequate or incompetent.
4. The opportunity to decline to carry out any actions they are uncomfortable about.
5. Removal of the negative consequences of failure, not seeking to apportion blame for mistakes.
6. An acceptance that short-term failure is necessary in order to produce long-term improvements.

It is possible to develop a coaching relationship that works purposefully towards goals that are relevant to the objectives of the sponsors of the coaching programme and that acknowledges the role of feelings and emotions. Acknowledging the role of feelings and emotions in the coaching process enables coaches to help people face challenges they might otherwise avoid, to find the right level of challenge when planning action and to make use of failures as well as successes. This is not intended to suggest that coaching is a therapeutic setting for the exploration of personal issues and feelings. This approach aims to help people manage, control and make positive use of their feelings and emotions in order to learn from situations which they find difficult or challenging.

Challenging deeply held beliefs and assumptions
Gillian Hill

This technique can be useful when a client has been working with you for a while, has started to make progress and is feeling safe in the mentoring relationship. She may express an assumption with absolute finality: 'Oh no, I couldn't do that' or 'Well, that would never happen'. The clues you are given that a deeply held belief has been stated are the certainty of her tone of voice and that words such as 'never', 'always', 'everyone' are said or implied, plus the use of injunctions, such as 'could/should/ought' or 'couldn't/shouldn't/oughtn't'. Your aim is then to help the client focus on the assumption until the underlying core belief becomes apparent.

The technique derives from the cognitive therapies and works on the theory that our thoughts are the basis of our behaviour and feelings, so, if we work out what our thoughts really are, we have an opportunity to change them and thus to change our behaviour and feelings.

Case study   Andrea

The client may say something like, 'I am permanently exhausted and snowed under at work but I couldn't possibly ask my manager for an assistant'. Because it is so self-evident to her, as are all assumptions, she may then move on to a different subject or be lost in contemplation of the hopelessness of the situation.

It is good then to flag up that you are going to help her examine this statement by saying something that brings her back to it, such as 'Let's stay with that and examine it a bit further'. If appropriate, you could draw attention to the finality of the statement by saying something such as 'Well, that's that then; no point in looking at *that* any further' if you can do it in a way that makes both of you smile and shows her the defeatism of her belief. This can reduce tension, and enable her to stand back from the belief and look at it more dispassionately, rather than being buried in the feelings that the belief engenders.

You could ask her to repeat the sentence as she might already have forgotten what she said. Repeat it yourself and then add 'Because' or 'Because, what would happen if you did…?' When she replies, just say 'And then, what would happen?' or 'And then, what would you feel?', until she has reached the core belief.

This could be something like 'People will realize I am useless'. Because the core belief causes such anxiety before it is discovered – which explains why a comfortable assumption is created to conceal it – they will try to deflect themselves on to another subject. Your aim is to be gently relentless:

You can't do that because…
So, what would happen if…
And then, what would happen…
And then…
And then you would feel…
Ah, so is that the real fear?

You never deny or refute their belief because that stops the process of teasing it out. It will only come out when you create a supportive environment where it is safe for anything to be said, no matter how trivial or how enormous.

Along the way, use as few words as possible so that you become just a prompt and they do not have to abandon their train of thought to focus on understanding what you are saying. If you can keep it to 'because', 'and then', 'and then', 'he would think what?', so much the better.

Once the core belief has been stated, let it hang in the air. Do not rush to fill the silence as sometimes a pause can produce, 'Well, if *that* is the problem, I know how to handle it.' Similarly, do not rush to provide options as the client may need first to assimilate the new idea.

Do not use this approach with someone until a solid working relationship has been established as it can be challenging and could be felt as threatening.

For the same reason, it is not for use with someone that you can tell is fragile. They need to be robust enough to reach the finishing line of their final realization or core belief. It is important that the client feels that you are on their side, gently chivvying them to a realization they are ready to make and can cope with. So, do not use it with anyone who wants to fix you in an opposing or authoritarian role.

Finally, ensure you do not undertake this approach in the closing moments of a session as you both need time to process the realization and/or to get back on to an easier, low-anxiety footing with each other before the end of the session.

The meaning of 'yes'

The meaning of 'yes' is a simple technique to test commitment. It asks the learner to be as candid as possible about where, on Figure 9.1, their level of commitment lies. Based on the response, they can explore with the mentor how much effort should be put into this issue.

10	I am totally determined to achieve this whatever the cost
9	I am very determined to do this and I'm prepared to make major sacrifices to do so
8	I will make this my number one priority
7	This will be one of my key priorities
6	It's very important to me
5	It's quite important to me
4	I feel obligated to do this
3	I'm not sure this is what I really want
2	I'm quite reluctant
1	Over my dead body!

Figure 9.1 The meaning of 'yes'.

Case study   **Angela**

Angela is an intelligent, resourceful woman in her late twenties, working for a distribution company. In her two latest appraisals, her manager pinpointed one major, specific area of weakness – teamworking. While her colleagues respect her for the quality of the work she does, they find her aloof and poor at sharing information. 'It is as if she is only concerned about getting her parts of the task done, and to hell with how the rest of us are doing', complained one of them. After each appraisal, she had made some efforts to be more collaborative, but soon relapsed into her habitual, insular style. After her line manager indicated strongly that he was getting exasperated and that the issue would have a substantial impact on her annual bonus, she raised the issue with her mentor.

When asked about her level of commitment, Angela's initial response was that it was quite high – somewhere between 6 and 7. When pressed to detail what that meant, however, she quickly changed to a 4 at best. The truth was, she liked working on her own, she hated having to explain things to people less smart than herself and, anyway, she was expecting shortly to move to another job in the same organization – so it seemed a waste of effort to build relationships with people she would probably never have to work with again.

The mentor helped her unpack each of these statements, looking for the assumptions behind them and challenging their validity. The new role did not require the same level of teamwork, but the mentor asked about the role she'd be promoted to from there, if she wanted to continue to progress in the organization. Yes, it would. Did she think that she had nothing to learn from her colleagues? No, they all had some knowledge or skills she could usefully tap into in her current role. What sort of reputation did she want to take with her into the new role?

Angela's level of commitment increased as she replaced the externally imposed reasons for improving her team-working competence with her own, internally generated, reasons for doing so. She and her mentor developed an action plan, which she worked at steadily for several months. When the expected job move came up, Angela turned it down, deciding that she would prefer to work in her current team, with whom she now had a much more fulfilling relationship.

Danger? What's dangerous about that?

It is very easy for mentees and coachees, particularly when under stress, to see the worst in a future situation that they have not thought through. This process is sometimes known as 'catastrophizing'.

| Case study | Nasser |

Our mentee, Nasser, was about to set up his own business, having spent many years working as a successful retail manager. One of his proposed business partners was also a friend, Lorraine. Lorraine was an intense, insightful individual, with training in Gestalt therapy and Psychosynthesis.

Both had been stressed by the pressure to start the business and other life events, and Nasser reported to his mentor that he experienced Lorraine as putting undue pressure on him, in fact so much so that it was dangerous. The mentor asked, 'Why was that dangerous?', and then took the answer and repeated the question. This continued and the sequence of responses went as follows:

- It is dangerous because I feel pressured.
- She is trying to psychoanalyse me.
- She takes things too far.
- She becomes critical of me.
- I end up worrying.
- It isn't dangerous at all – in fact it's useful!

Personal development planning

PSDP technique
Linda Phipps, Director, St. Williams's Foundation and a non-executive director in the NHS

The PSDP – Personal Skills Development Plan – is a deceptively simple but effective technique. It has been developed from 10 years of active involvement in coaching and mentoring as a simple but powerful tool for Personal Development Planning – PDP. It addresses the needs of people such as supervisors and managers in their early appointments, who have not previously had access to PDP, for an accessible and, above all, practical technique. It provides a guide to immediate action, and for longer-term action, and is tailored to individual needs.

It assumes the active support of a significant other. This can be a mentor or a line manager. It was developed originally in response to the needs of a group of supervisors to follow up and build on their first management training course, and it has been refined by much practical application since.

How does it work?
The PSDP technique is forward-focused, and is based on a 5-stage model. The first step in the approach is to define a future role/job that you or your mentee wish to develop towards.

The second step is to develop a list of the skills required in this role in discussion with the coachee or menteee.

The third stage is seeking to capture against each skill at least one example – evidence – of how the mentee demonstrated this. This is the hardest bit! This part is not about whether they possess this skill inherently. It is about being able to prove the successful delivery of an action or initiative that demonstrates this skill.

The fourth stage to consider is, where are the gaps? These will probably be of three types:

1. Areas where they have natural skills, but have not had a chance to demonstrate them.
2. Areas where they lack natural skills, and haven't had exposure to situations where they were needed.
3. Areas where they can demonstrate the skill, but it's not a good example.

So, fifthly, the gaps form the basis of an action plan – which focuses on developing demonstrable experience to capture in the right-hand column.

Case study   Charlie, the aspiring retail manager

Charlie wanted to become a retail manager. With his learning partner, he worked through what the skills that he would require were. I then acted as his mentor to facilitate teasing out good examples of skills he had already demonstrated. We could then easily see where the gaps were, and developed a phased action plan to get him good experience in these gap areas, for example, to create the opportunity for him to demonstrate leadership/participation in cross-functional teams and projects. As we often said, it wasn't necessarily about being naturally brilliant at everything – more about creating your own track record of being effective and competent across the range of skills you are likely to need.

Application

The PSDP technique has also been used by more experienced managers, as a useful way to prepare for appraisals, or to analyse training needs. Finally, this approach is useful in preparing for job applications and interviews, both those for which detailed criteria and specifications are spelt out, and those for which they are not – see English (2004). This approach can be applied to a specific application, and in preparing for being better placed to apply for a range of jobs at a future date.

It is not applicable as a general development model for more experienced managers and for those who have had plenty of sophisticated management training. It works best for those who are keen and motivated to learn, and by implication – as it requires a degree of effort by the individual to think of past and future examples of work – would work less well with the unmotivated. That said, because it is simple, effective, practical, and enables 'quick wins', it is potentially useful for working with those who are turned off by theory and 'management-speak'.

Planning is not enough

One of us worked as a mentor with a talented developer called Craig. He made some huge changes during the mentoring period, but, in spite of this, he was often frustrated with his own lack of progress. In reflecting about this later he wrote the following case.

Case study   **Craig's own case study**

Talking about squash coaching the other night made me reflect that 'head knowledge' is one thing but actually being able to do something is quite another. This is particularly true for me in squash since I know what I should be doing, but actually doing it during a game is another matter. I think this applies to all kinds of coaching: there is no shortage of advice and insights on what we are doing wrong. The problems invariably arise when we try to change our habits, whether it be procrastination, shying away from marketing oneself or chasing the ball into the corners of the court.

I am wondering if a really good coach would spend very little time faffing around with insights and motivations and lots of time dragging the coachee off to practise the skill/behaviour they are trying to master. Too many coaches say, 'Right, we've agreed you need to do X, now you go off and do it'. I've seen lots of people, including myself, turn up at the next session with some excellent, cast-iron reasons why the universe conspired against them in such a way that they couldn't possibly do X last time, but they promise they will do it next time. Sometimes we need someone to take us by the hand and lead us gently to the edge of our comfort zone, then stand there with us while we do things we might not have the courage to do otherwise. Another way putting this is to say that we need someone to drag us by the ear, kicking and screaming, to the edge of the comfort zone, then stand there with arms folded until we do what we said we wanted to do, refusing to allow us to go home for our tea until we've done it.

Many coaches will be tempted to analyse Craig's responses here and have lots of ways of talking him through his issues – dependency, trying to, counter-dependency, and so on. That is the point though – he knows about all this stuff; he just wants to stop chasing into those corners.

References

Donnison, P. A. (2000). *Images of Outdoor Management Development. A Synthesis of the Literature and Participants' Experiences on Outdoor Courses*. PhD dissertation, Department of Management Learning, Lancaster University.

English, P. (2004). *Succeeding at Interviews Pocketbook*. Alresford: Management Pocketbooks.

Megginson, D. and Whitaker, V. (2003). *Continuing Professional Development*. London: CIPD.

Murray, W. H. (2002). *The Evidence of Things not Seen: A Mountaineer's Tale*. London: Bâton Wicks.

Persaud, R. (2001). *Staying Sane: How to Make your Mind Work for You*. London: Bantam.

Vince, R. and Martin, L. (1993). Inside action learning: An exploration of the psychology and politics of the action learning model. In *Management Education and Development*, **24**(3), 205–15.

Whitmore, J. (2003). *Coaching for Performance: GROWing People, Performance and Purpose*, 3rd edn. London: Nicholas Brealey.

Yerkes, R. M. and Dodson, J. D. (1908). The relative strength of stimulus to rapidity of habit formation. *Journal of Comparative Neurology and Psychology*, **18**, 459–82.

Chapter 10

Managing the learner's own behaviour

Introduction

Dr Johnson famously said:

> He who has so little knowledge of human nature as to seek happiness by changing anything but his own disposition will waste his life in fruitless effort.

His prescription was to focus our change efforts on ourselves. Much of the effort of coaching and mentoring can follow his direction. This can be particularly valuable to coachees and mentees in frozen bureaucracies where the prospects of organizational change are slim.

There are four techniques described in this chapter. The first two use focus to provide insight and an impulse to change. *Culpable vagueness* helps learners to move from general statements to a clarity about what they want to do. *Transforming vices into virtues* uses appreciative inquiry to help learners to see the value in a habit and to overcome its dark side. The other two techniques are depth approaches for experienced helpers, working in an established relationship. *Confronting – mentoring beyond challenging* is Julian Lippi's approach to unfreezing stuck behaviour patterns. *Exaggeration* is a technique we have used on occasion to enhance the will to change by seeing a habit through to its logical (and emotional) conclusion.

Change through focus and attention

The first two techniques are helpful in focusing the learner on paying attention to their own behaviour.

Culpable vagueness

Some Buddhists suggest that there is a kind of vagueness that represents a moral position that can be criticized. This is when we use vagueness deliberately to avoid doing what we know needs doing. One way that mentees and coachees can do this is by keeping their intentions general. In these cases the coach or mentor can help by getting specific.

Case study   **Andy, ambulance service inspector**

Andy said that he needed to get on with developing his contribution to his highly bureaucratic service. When he was pressed on this he said, 'I need to work on developing my Job Description.' His coach asked, 'What specifically?' He then replied, 'Well, I've got a problem with my boss'. This seemed strikingly different from the original formulation, and a potentially rich area for action, so the coach asked again, 'What specifically?' He then raised aspects of his boss's behaviour and talked about their impact on the service. Again this seemed to be going away from Andy and what he might do about it, so the coach asked, 'What does this difficulty raise about you?' At this point, Andy had an agenda that he could work on directly, which he did.

Transforming vices into virtues

This technique uses Appreciative Inquiry methods (Srivastva and Cooperrider, 1990) to address what is viewed as a problem by a 2 stage process. First, build self-acceptance by helping the player to look at the positive side of the vice and, secondly, find and use a strength from elsewhere in the player's life to build a solution based on what he already knows.

Case study   **Brian's supervision session**

Brian, a senior sales manager, said that he realized that, often in his own coaching, he was less effective than he wanted to be because of his impatience. It made him behave in a driven way (as he did with his own job) and push his coachees into setting demanding targets with short timescales for completion, regardless of workload. He found that sometimes this energized his coachees, but often it just made them back off and reduce commitment to working for a desired outcome.

In supervision sessions, Brian was encouraged to think of all the advantages of this vice of his; how it worked well for him; others who had valued it; how it was good even for those who resented it. So the first point to establish was that he need not beat himself up for this quality, which was simply his way – with advantages and disadvantages.

He was then asked to think of occasions when the quality of impatience risked knocking him off course in aspects of his life other than work, and what he did about them there to use the positives and not to be distracted by the negatives.

He identified martial arts as an area where he had developed ways of handling impatience. He said that what he did when he felt this impatience (with himself as a learner in this case) coming on, was to take a deep breath, relax and focus on the result he wanted to achieve. He then used his martial arts technique to centre himself in his coaching sessions whenever he felt his impatience rising.

Deep challenge in words and action

Neither of these activities is for the faint-hearted. Both are best used by experienced helpers in the context of a strong and established relationship. In these circumstances they can have powerful effects where less powerful techniques might fail.

Confronting – mentoring beyond challenging
Julian Lippi

Effective mentoring is about creating opportunities for developing insights that lead to major changes or transitions in how people think, how they operate, and what they know. For this to happen mentoring partners need to be able to take the risk to work outside of the operating area where they feel comfortable. This applies just as much to the mentor as it does to the person with whom they are working.

One of the highest risk taking approaches for a mentor is confronting. Not to be confused with challenging (a normal almost day-to-day part of any learning relationship), confronting is about taking a risk to work at the very limits of a relationship – that zone where if things are pushed too far, the relationship could be damaged or come apart.

Confronting can be a useful approach to take when the mentee is really stuck. Being stuck happens for a variety of reasons – having a major blind spot on an issue, recognizing there is an issue but taking 'evasive action', being 'paralysed' by an issue, and so forth. Under these circumstances, supporting or challenging to try and get someone to engage with the issue does not result in them gaining all the insight they need to deal with the issue effectively.

For some while I had been using some confrontation with both groups and individuals when I came across Frank Farrelly and Jeff Brandsma's work *Provocative Therapy*. While this book is about psychotherapy, it gave me a better framework to understand the role of confrontation in a supportive mentoring relationship. Very simply, their approach involves using confrontation with a light touch – they recommend humour – to move the person from an 'I cannot' mindset in relation to the problem or issue to a position of accepting some responsibility for what's happening, 'I will not'. Once the person has accepted responsibility for their part of the issue they can begin to take action to bring about a change in their behaviour.

Case study   Georgia

A client and I had been focusing on changing some unhelpful behavioural patterns that had developed in her relationship with her CEO that were having a negative impact on her ability to function effectively. For over 2 years Georgia had worked diligently and painstakingly on thinking about problems and issues differently and changing behaviour which did not appear to be helping her in her situation. She experimented with different ways of framing issues and different ways of doing things. With my help she systematically reflected on her experience and attempted to put her insights into action.

Despite having made great progress in most areas she remained stuck around the issue of how to work with her CEO. This had a lot to do with the dysfunctional operating style of her boss and that was exactly where Georgia was stuck. She kept developing strategies to try to change him to improve the relationship. What she found was that the first Newtonian Law of Physics (that action and reaction are equal and opposite) also applies in organizations. The more she pushed, the more he pushed back. The frustration of having to deal with a loose cannon of a boss who resented having to make decisions and punished anyone whom he felt had forced him to make one, led to an almost constant stream of anger and tears for Georgia. It was as if every great stride she had made to change her circumstances was negated by this man's intransigence.

When we met for breakfast at a small restaurant Georgia was quite happy with the progress she'd been making. She had been using a model I had suggested to help her focus her energy into areas where she had control or influence and could actually make things happen. That's what she believed she was doing, anyway. We had covered the ground a number of times before and the fact of the matter was that she was fooling herself. She was well and truly stuck and was putting most of her energy into the wrong areas — generally into areas where she could not make things change and so she was just banging her head against brick walls, and then, because she'd wasted all her will and energy, giving up in areas where she could actually have made a difference.

Because of her fragility I had been working with her gently, supporting most of the time and challenging whenever possible. I had thought of going further on a number of occasions, but it had not felt right and I always stopped short of going past challenging into confronting. On this day our conversation focused almost exclusively on the 4-quadrant model she was using to help her leverage her effort. It was crystal clear to me (as I had suspected on past occasions), that, despite her enthusiasm for the model, there was one quadrant that she never mentioned. It was undiscussable. It was as if it did not exist even though there it was right in front of us on the page.

Giving up

Giving up in the model represented the areas where Georgia was in control and could take action but for whatever reason chose not to take action and instead gave up. Throughout her life, the one thing you could not have accused her of doing was giving up. She had been a tenacious fighter no matter what the odds, an attitude I suspect she'd learned in part from a prizefighting grandfather. So why was she giving up now on so many things?

As our conversation continued, I focused more and more on what I thought might happen if I confronted her with what I believed she was doing. I knew from our long relationship that it would not be good, but I wasn't quite sure of the exact reaction. I was convinced that no matter what happened as a consequence of me 'calling it' and confronting her with her demons, our relationship was strong and elastic enough to withstand whatever happened — just strong enough, but that's all you need.

She stopped talking and I said 'What about the Giving Up quadrant? There must be something there. Everyone gives up sometimes.' The relaxed warmth in her face drained away. For a moment there was iciness and then anger, pure anger. She said nothing and I feared she would start yelling and storm out of the restaurant. Immediately I started thinking that perhaps this hadn't been the right moment to start to confront after all. I paid the bill and suggested we walk for a while. Eventually we began to talk about the issues, the anger, and the lack of action in areas where she was clearly in control of taking action.

Georgia later told me that my confrontation had provoked a murderous rage, but that the conversation was a watershed. Giving up on things that were achievable was anathema to her. When I had raised the issue she found it profoundly confronting and disturbing because it went against her idea of who she was and how she worked. I had scratched at the surface of something

(Continued)

that she knew deep down was happening, but couldn't bring herself to admit. She had been giving up on some very important things while kidding herself that it was constructive to waste time and energy on things she couldn't change.

Following my confronting her Georgia accepted responsibility for her behaviour and set about changing it. In a short time she began to operate in ways that were significantly different and when she realized that she had got about as far as anyone could get with her boss she made plans and moved on.

A glaring error I made on the day was that, having confronted, I kept pushing her during our subsequent conversation. In feedback she gave to me later, Georgia reported feeling 'battered and bruised by the experience'. She told me that it would have been better if I had just supported her as she absorbed what I had confronted her with rather than keeping on 'at her'. It raises an important aspect of confronting. Because the consequences of confronting can be so grave, it needs to be used lightly and deftly, even humorously, but with clear support offered after the confronting.

In mentoring you should not resort to confrontation too early. The mentor contemplating confronting needs to be absolutely sure that the person they are working with is stuck in a way that merits taking such profound action. It is a technique of last resort which should never be used early in a relationship and should only be used when the relationship is robust enough to withstand the possible negative consequences.

Confronting should never be used unless you are absolutely certain that you are doing it to help the person. If for whatever reason the mentor is feeling frustrated or negative about the person, especially if the latter is annoyed or angry, it is not appropriate to confront.

The final test for using confronting in mentoring must always be: 'If I confront them with this will it help them to get unstuck or move us to another level where they might begin to get unstuck?' If the answer to the question is yes and you feel you have the experience, confidence and enough time to process the aftermath of the confrontation, then and only then, you should move to confronting.

Exaggeration

Some behaviours and deeply embedded in individuals' repertoires, and no amount of discussion will lead to lasting change. In these circumstances, it can sometimes be helpful to encourage the learner to exaggerate the behaviour and to see what that feels like. The composite case study of Bill offers our experience of using this high-risk, high-energy technique.

Case study   Bullying Bill

Bill is a senior manager in a pharmaceutical company. Through upward and peer appraisal, he had been made aware of a number of behaviours which created a climate of fear among those people who reported to him. He was prone to bursts of temper and he tended to dominate meetings. If he didn't agree with a point someone else was making, he would show his impatience, fidgeting with a pen and breathing heavily. His direct reports learnt to assess his opinion early on in a discussion and fall in line. This lack of dissent was interpreted by Bill as a sign of cohesion and team strength.

When he received feedback about what was actually going on in his colleagues' minds, he was shocked and committed himself to change his behaviours. A coach was appointed to help him, but it soon became clear that his commitment was only surface deep. Although, when shadowed by the coach for a day, he did make an attempt to engage and listen, after half an hour or so of a meeting, the prevailing habits showed through and by the afternoon he was clearly no longer trying to restrain himself.

The coach tackled the problem initially by trying to understand the underlying beliefs on which he was operating. These boiled down to the following:

- There's never enough time to get things done, so it's my job to stop people wasting time in pointless debate.
- I have a very clear idea of what my own boss wants us to achieve and I'm paid to make sure people fall into line with those objectives.
- This is the way I've always operated and I've always got results; I'm too old (he was 44) to change now.

The coach also asked him about what he enjoyed about his job. Among his key responses were 'Winning and getting my own way'. *What's the difference between that and being a bully?*, asked the coach. Although offended by the question, Bill tried hard to answer it. Eventually, at an intellectual level, at least, he accepted that colleagues could perceive his behaviour as bullying. Once again, he committed himself to making some changes.

In practice, the first few desultory attempts quickly faded away. When he invited his direct reports to say what they really thought, none had the courage (or stupidity) to do so. That was all the excuse he needed to go back to his previous behaviour.

The key that unlocked the door for Bill was a high-risk strategy, which the coach adopted in desperation. 'All right,' said the coach, 'let's accept that your underlying beliefs are justified and appropriate. Why don't you play them out fully? Why not shout at people all the time and tell them openly

(Continued)

that their opinions are rubbish?' As he and Bill explored this scenario, it became clear that the only real restraining force was fear of what Bill's own bosses would say and do if he went to that extreme.

'Well, I want you to try doing just that for the next week,' said the coach. 'If I clear it with your boss and the HR director, will you try that?' After some hesitation, Bill agreed he would, although he was beginning to doubt the coach's sanity.

When it came to the crunch, however, Bill found he just couldn't do it. He saw that he was acting as a gross parody of himself. So much so that after less than a day, he made a point of apologizing to his entire team — something he'd never done before. This acting out of the caricature of himself stuck with him far more effectively than any of the previous discussions and exhortation had done. He now began actively to work at not being the awful person of the extreme. After a while he gained enough confidence to commission a drawing depicting the monster he could have become and placing it on his office wall as a reminder. In the end, it was the negative image that gave Bill the depth of emotional commitment to change his behaviour.

References

Farrelly, F. and Bradsma, J. (1974). *Provocative Therapy*. Cupertino, California: Meta Publications.

Srivastva, S. and Cooperrider, D. L. (eds) (1990). *Appreciative Management and Leadership: The Power of Positive Thought and Action in Organizations*. San Francisco: Jossey-Bass.

Chapter 11

Building support, influence and learning

Introduction

Mentors can from time to time provide access to powerful others from whom the mentee can benefit, but this approach is relatively rare in European developmental mentoring and is often frowned upon as being corrosive of equal opportunity (Megginson, 2000). Instead, building support and influence is best seen as a task for the mentee, and we offer a framework technique for this in the first section, called *Fitting into the mentee's network*. We describe a technique based around *Revans' questions*, and give a case study of its use. Peter Matthews, of Ernst & Young, offers a technique that he calls *Who would want to network with me?* because he finds people are inhibited from networking for their own purposes by a deeply held belief about needing to be helpful to others rather than have them help you. We also present a model from our own work, on motivation for networking.

   The second section looks at techniques for building learning – particularly *Keeping a log of learning*. We also have a summary technique on *Note taking during sessions*.

Building support and influence

Fitting into the mentee's network

This technique is about how the coach or mentor fits into the network of other influencers of the coachee. This is the opposite way round from the

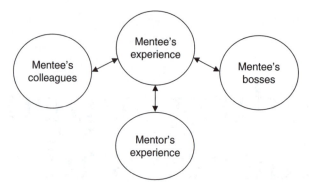

Figure 11.1   Mentee's influences.

way in which the issue is often presented – certainly in the US mentoring literature (Megginson, 2000). In the US literature, sponsorship is an issue, and the mentor is the one with the rich influence map, which is displayed to the eager mentee who can use it to further their career.

Looking at the issue from the coachee's perspective, they will be influenced by their own experience and by the experience and perspective of a variety of others. The problem for the coach or mentor is to assess who these people are, what their influence is and how that influence is applied.

For the coach, one of the resources is feedback from watching the learners interact with these people – but even that is limited to specific situations and a finite number of key influencers. 360° feedback (and other forms of appraisal) of the coachee or mentee can fill in some gaps, but the coach has to be wary of the different purposes for which this data is collected. Ultimately, it is up to the learner to develop their own network, and the helper can contribute by asking questions such as:

- Who has a clear perspective on how you're doing in this area?
- Whose opinion do you trust and value on this?
- What would they say?
- Who knows about this aspect of your desired career?
- Who else could you ask about this?
- What would be your dream list of helpers on this matter?

Further details on analysing and developing networks is given in Megginson and Whitaker, 2003, p. 111–14.

Revans' questions

Reg Revans, the inventor of action learning (Revans, 1998), has long advised the use of three questions in helping learners to work out who they need to talk with. These are:

1. Who knows?
2. Who can?
3. Who cares?

The answer to the first gives the learner sources for the *information* they need. The answer to the second considers the dimension of *power*. In developing myself or my performance or my organization, it is useful to consider who has the power to make a difference to outcomes. Who do I have to get on-side if I want to achieve these outcomes? Finally there is the issue of *will*. Who is there who shares my concerns and wants to do something about it?

Case study   David coaches Phil

Phil was a director of a high-profile national public body. He was deeply frustrated that the executive board of the organization was ineffectual. In fact he thought it was dysfunctional, in that it was criss-crossed with resentments, rivalries and hidden agendas. Phil felt very alone in his concern about this. By using Revans' questions, David helped Phil to focus down on people in the board who did have an agenda for improvement, and who, like him, currently felt powerless. He also identified non-executives and others in related bodies who had a stake in making things different. Armed with this insight he developed a plan to do something about what had, up until then, seemed a hopeless and lonely task.

Who would want to network with me?
Peter Matthews, Ernst & Young

One has to ask the questions 'Why?' and 'How?' to fully understand the power of building effective networks.

Helping with the 'why?'
Ask the helpee to think about how to solve a problem outside their work (e.g. the need to repair something at home). They usually go through a list of who they know who could help. I keep challenging: 'Suppose you didn't know anybody who knew? What would you do then?' We start to draw a diagram with lots of links and nodes back to the original person – friends of friends, contacts of friends, business contacts, and very soon we have a large number of names on the paper. We talk about the consequences and benefits of having that type of network and what it would therefore mean for the individual. Very often by taking it away from

work (sometimes people think it can be 'political' to build networks at work) it helps show, in a less politically charged context, some of the benefits of network generation.

A transition is made into work and we discuss how a complex problem might be solved and how many people potentially one might need in order to solve the problem. The link can then be made to how an individual gains skills and the degree to which any one person has the skills and knowledge that they will need to help them achieve their development plan.

Helping with the 'how'?

In truth I think I spend far more time working on the 'how' than the 'why'. How do you make that call to introduce yourself to someone? How do others do it?

This is where a mentor can play an enormous role. I have heard this described as a generator of resourcefulness. The mentor can explore the 'how' in a number of ways.

- Make direct contact themselves.
- Helping coach the individual through what they are going to say when they make the call.
- Helping the individual think about the benefits of what they might give in return for developing a new relationship (there tends to be a strong belief that it is wrong to 'exploit' others and people aren't good at articulating what it is they offer in return).
- Helping people cope with how individuals might feel if you ask them to introduce them to one of their contacts (again people tend to over-estimate the feelings).
- Helping people think outside the box in terms of what they could build (e.g. if you are trying to build a network of people who understand the future of a business sector, then it won't just be businesses themselves, but might be analysts, bankers, accountants, lawyers, business advisers, university professors).

Because I spend so much time helping people cope with the belief about how much value they can add to others – i.e. What's in it for the other party? – I call this technique, 'Who would want to network with me?'

What do I want to network for?

The matrix (Figure 11.2) below illustrates the different reasons people network. Motivations for networking may be anchored in the present or the future; or in the needs either to gain influence (for example, people who can help you make things happen) or to acquire information (for

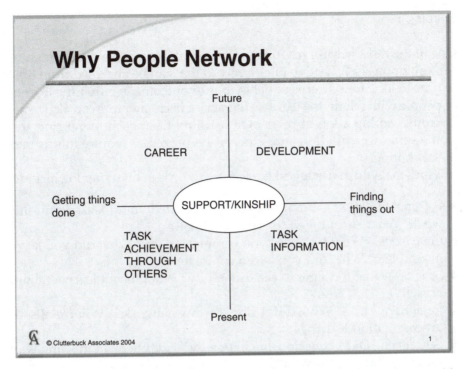

Figure 11.2   Exploring what the client is looking for through networking can provide both focus and a more comprehensive approach.

example, finding out about new job opportunities or new concepts). The five motivations that emerge from these two dimensions are:

- *Task information* – what you need to know to be effective in your current roles
- *Task achievement* – support in doing your current roles
- *Career* – Linking with people who can play an active role in furthering your career objectives
- *Development* – meeting people who can help with your personal growth
- *Mutual support/kinship* – the comfort and confidence that comes from knowing that there are other people who share the same issues and concerns as you do, and who can offer mutual help and learning.

Building learning

Learning is maximized in one-to-one helping by processes such as learning logs and journals. Creative writing can also be used in this way (Bolton, 2001). Autobiographical stories are also helpful here, and are discussed in other chapters.

Keeping a log

One of the most helpful resources a learner and his or her coach–mentor can call upon is a reflective log – a record that can be analysed from time to time to look for patterns of behaviour or outcome in either the learner or people with whom the learner interacts. Coach–mentors can also benefit from keeping a log of their own learning from each mentoring session – some accreditation and supervision processes require this as part of the routine.

Issues that you may suggest the learner records in his or her log include:

- *Personal fulfilment* – What has really frustrated you/pleased you this week? What encouraged/discouraged you?
- *Completion* – What tasks did you complete today? What did you leave incomplete? What did you avoid completely?
- *Insight* – What did I get to see differently? What have I learned about myself?
- *Resourcefulness* – Who did I add to my networks? What skills or processes did I learn?
- *Behaviour* – Did I consciously change the way I behave in some way today? What was the result?
- *Goal fulfilment* – What did I do today to take me towards longer-term goals?
- *Decisions* – What significant decisions did I make today? How do I feel about them?
- *Challenge* – Who or what did I challenge today?

The data from these records have a number of valuable functions. First, they focus the learner's mind on the goals she or he wants to achieve. Secondly, they frequently reveal recurrent patterns, which can be further analysed with a view to changing them. Thirdly, they provide a rich vein of material for dialogue. And fourthly, many learners find it useful to look back at their logs 6 months or a year later and review just how much progress they have made.

Case study   **Alan's frustration and success log**

Alan is chief executive of an organization in the National Health Service. He asked for a mentor because this was his first CEO role and he wanted someone to help him think through political problems, which he was unfamiliar with. His mentor asked him to keep a log of frustrations and successes, which he did for 6 weeks, before presenting it for discussion. The discussion quickly focused on a series of incidents where he had felt frustrated with the chairman, or sensed that the chairman was annoyed with him. The mentor helped him look for common themes in these events, occasionally suggesting an interpretation, which Alan was able either to accept or reject.

One overriding theme emerged from the frustrations – they all occurred around activities, where the boundaries of responsibility between Alan and his chairman were blurred. Conversely, most of the successful encounters with the chairman were in situations where responsibilities were clearly defined. From here, it was relatively simple to design tactics for gaining greater role clarity.

Alan eventually met with the chairman to set down clearer rules of engagement. Although this eased the problem, the chairman from time to time breached this agreement. Recording his frustrations still, Alan was able to explore new tactics with the mentor, keeping the problem in check, although it was never fully solved until the chairman moved on. With his new chairperson, Alan took the initiative and established responsibilities and ground-rules from day one; setting expectations from the beginning made for a much easier and mutually supportive relationship.

Note taking during sessions

In the previous technique we considered the notes that the helper or learner might take *between* sessions. In this technique we turn our attention to the interesting issue of writing things down *during* meetings. We list below arguments for and against helpers and learners taking notes.

Learner takes notes
For:

- Places responsibility with learner for using and acting on what is discussed.
- Empowers the learner to choose what they want to take from the conversation.

Against:

- May distract the learner from thinking about their issues.
- Reduces spontaneity.

Helper takes notes
For:

- A service to the learner – helper can send polished notes to the learner later as a reminder.
- Useful for helper in preparing for the next meeting with the learner.

Against:

- May mean that the helper misses non-verbal cues by focusing on what is being written.
- Learner may feel a loss of empathic connection with the helper, and in some circumstances note taking can be downright intimidating.

Practices for minimizing disadvantages and maximizing benefits
We have found that the following responses to note taking can be helpful:

- Make an agreement at the beginning of the relationship about who will take notes and for what purposes.
- Differentiate notes as reminders, notes for action, notes for sharing and private notes for oneself.
- If appropriate, take a brief pause from talking for one or both parties to make notes.
- Consider using techniques in which note taking, drawing or constructing other representations is integral to the technique itself.
- Be prepared to suggest that it might be an idea to make a note at various points in the discussion.
- Make notes at key stages, particularly when exploring a range of options, making a decision, or preparing a plan.

References

Bolton, G. (2001). *Reflective Practice: Writing and Professional Development.* London: Paul Chapman.

Megginson, D. (2000). Current issues in mentoring. *Career Development International,* **5**(4–5), 256–60.

Megginson, D. and Whitaker, V. (2003). *Continuing Professional Development.* London: CIPD.

Revans, R. (1998). *The ABC of Action Learning.* London: Lemos & Crane.

Chapter 12

Ending the relationship

Introduction

In Clutterbuck and Megginson, 2004, we describe research we undertook into ending mentoring relationships. We found that relationships could either be wound down – where they fell into disuse; or wound up – where they were concluded deliberately.

The experience of Peter Matthews of Ernst & Young illustrates the difficulties of this stage in mentoring and offers some practices to minimize the difficulties.

An issue that occurs at the end of, but also throughout, the relationship is that of reviewing. There is a great temptation at the end of a session as time is running out to focus on future plans; so it is well to review previous meetings at the start of the next one. This can be done briefly at every meeting, or a bigger review can be held every three or so meetings. A collective case study of the power of review is given later in this chapter in *Defining relationship success*.

Winding up/winding down relationships

Thoughts on winding up and winding down
Peter Matthews (Ernst & Young)

The distinction between mentors and coaches is actually quite important. My experience of mentoring relationships (either as a mentor or mentee) have led me believe it is harder in mentoring to retain the 'power in the relationship', than it is in coaching. Mentoring relationships can lead to dependence and, at worst, parent–child dynamics.

I suspect people often see letting go as an emotionally difficult subject, which is why so many mentoring relationships just drift on.

I was once a mentor in a professional services environment where there was an end goal. It was clearly articulated that our relationship would change at the point the end game was reached. Throughout the mentoring relationship we were both very up-front about what it was we were seeking to achieve and how the relationship would change over a period of time.

Even so it is not easy. I know of one situation in Ernst & Young where someone was being mentored through to partnership. The former mentee is now the boss of the mentor and feels extremely uncomfortable to the point where he has sub-contracted some of the personal counselling/coaching required.

Winding down comes down to two issues:

- the nature of the contract set up front;
- the degree to which mentor and mentee are prepared to review the living contract as the relationship evolves.

Time, breakdowns, tensions and differing personal agendas tend to suggest that it can be very easy for relationships to drift apart. Sometimes a mentee might lack confidence in the face of a more senior or powerful figure. My experience of mentor–mentee relationships is that they tend to start with a flourish, launched by a programme, but tend to die over a fairly short period of time.

This be avoided by ensuring the following:

- A clear contract about how and when the relationship might end.
- Willingness to revisit and change the contract.
- A sense of two-way benefit. As mentor, I have found I gain as much as the mentee by asking for feedback on my skills and from being encouraged to seek new insights by the mentee.
- Willingness to confront issues as they occur, particularly when things are getting difficult.

Review

Defining relationship success

One of the most confining things a coach or mentor can do is to limit discussion about desired outcomes to the learner's set goals. By focusing instead on goals for the relationship, the coach–mentor opens up a wide vista of opportunities to enhance the value and quality of the time the two people have together. It is useful to explore what both parties would like to get out of the relationship, in terms of:

- career outcomes (e.g. achieving a new position);
- capability outcomes (e.g. improving or acquiring a key skill);
- enabling (e.g. feeling more confident, having a clearer career plan).

It is important not to promise too much, or create expectations that all these desired outcomes will occur to a significant degree (though it is surprising how often this does seem to be the case in relationships that achieve both depth and longevity). Prioritizing the outcomes helps the learner be realistic in his or her expectations and helps focus both parties' dialogue in subsequent meetings. It also encourages the review process, in which helper and learner periodically summarize for each other what they have gained from the relationship and how its impact could be enhanced.

Clearly defining success, at the start of the relationship, can mean that emotional issues of ending are minimized. If the parties have set realistic goals, and have worked towards them steadily, then ending becomes an obvious and natural process.

Case study

Some years ago, one of the authors was facilitating a mentoring scheme for a public sector employer. There were just over 50 pairs and virtually all participants turned up for a review session. When they were asked what they had gained from the relationship, virtually everyone was enthusiastic. However, when asked what they thought the other party had gained, they mostly admitted they had no idea and many felt guilty they were taking so much and giving so little. When they did share their thoughts and experiences, they were surprised at the extent to which the flow of benefit was two-way. From then on, many of these relationships strengthened in both intensity and quality of outcome to the participants.

Reference

Clutterbuck, D. and Megginson, D. (2004). All good things must come to an end: winding up and winding down a mentoring relationship. In *The Situational Mentor* (Clutterbuck, D. and Lane, G., eds). Aldershot: Gower.

Chapter 13

Building your own techniques

Introduction

Most of the tools described in this book have come about because we (or other people) have been in situations where our ability to help someone else reflect and understand has been stretched. Sometimes we have responded by asking the learner for permission to experiment, to take a new path without any clear idea of where it is leading. When we do so, we are creating mutual learning, but also mutual risk – as coaches and mentors we need to maintain a deep awareness of and sensitivity to boundaries and, in particular, to our own limitations.

At other times, new techniques and approaches emerge from our reflections on our failures or partial successes. How could I have helped more effectively? What would have shifted the ground of our dialogue sufficiently to permit genuinely new thinking? What could I have said that would have made a difference?

In this chapter we list *Some key questions to ask in developing new techniques* and we emphasize the value of *Recording new approaches* and of *Having a store of good questions*. We conclude this chapter with three brief techniques that help to leverage further techniques. These are called *Focus on the learner*, *Up and down the ladder* and *Fix the learning*.

Developing your own library of techniques

Coaches and mentors grow by experimenting; both with techniques devised by others and with approaches they design and test themselves. How they do so is as much a measure of their ability in the role as how they conduct the sessions they have with those they help.

Key steps in the development and maintenance of professional capability include the following:

- *Having and maintaining their own learning agenda.*
- *Maintaining a learning log, in which they record challenges, concepts and new approaches arising from their practice as coach or mentor.*
- *Sharing challenges and new approaches with professional colleagues (e.g. in a supervision group).*

Exposing experimental approaches to experienced colleagues is an important part of the process. Effective supervision provides an opportunity to identify approaches others have used, to explore better ways of using familiar techniques and to share new approaches with others who can offer constructive criticism and ideas.

Some key questions to ask in developing new techniques

The following questions are ones that we have found generative in developing techniques for this book, and in our own professional practice:

- What is the barrier I have encountered?
- How does it differ from issues I have tackled before?
- Why does the learner find it difficult to deal with?
- Why do I find it difficult to help?
- Whose benefit is this approach for? Whose agenda does it address?
- What are the risks and dangers of this approach? Have I explored these with the learner? What's the worst that can happen if it doesn't work?
- Is this approach really likely to move things along?
- Am I straying into areas beyond my competence?
- Have I exhausted my existing store of techniques?
- Have I engaged the learner in thinking of new ways to tackle the issue?
- How can I capture the core of this approach so I can repeat it?
- How and when will I reflect upon the approach?
- How will I evaluate its effectiveness? (Can I obtain relevant feedback from the learner? Is there some way of gaining third-party feedback?)

Recording new approaches

One of the disappointments in the early stages of writing this book was our discovery that so few coaches and mentors bothered to capture their learning about different approaches and techniques. Many of the contributions we received in our first trawl were no more than vague descriptions of theory drawn from elsewhere and an assumption that simply being aware of theory was enough to promote appropriate questions. The idea of developing an individual library of techniques and recording experience in using each was far less widespread than we had imagined.

Perhaps we should not have been surprised at the lack of articulation of practice. It was a finding in one of our doctoral theses (Megginson (1999), pp. 304–14) that one feature that differentiated intellectual property developers in management development from others in the field, was just this tendency to crystallize their experience. A message of this book is that we can all become intellectual property developers now.

Having a store of good questions

In addition to maintaining a personal library of techniques, we also recommend building your own library of good coaching questions. We call them MDQs (Massively Difficult Questions) because they oblige the learner to pause and reflect, and examine issues, at a level well below the normal surface response. The following section, *107 great coaching and mentoring questions*, is extracted from our own libraries of MDQs.

We have collected these questions from various sources and have alphabetized them for this list. Notice the predominance of 'How,' 'What' and 'Who' questions, and the relative scarcity of 'Why.' 'Why' takes us up into abstraction, whereas 'How,' 'What' and 'Who' takes us to the specific and concrete. What is the emphasis in your own list?

107 Great coaching and mentoring questions

1. Are there any emotions you are trying to avoid here?
2. By how much do you want to improve, by when?
3. Could you treat this as an experiment and see what happens between now and our next meeting?
4. Do you dread the conversation with X? What's causing that feeling? How might that emotion affect whether you achieve the outcome you want?
5. Do you need to control this situation? If so, why?
6. How committed are you to achieving this?
7. How could you find the courage to do what you think is right?
8. How could you have done this better?

9. How do you like to be managed?
10. How does this fit in with your personal values?
11. How genuinely committed are you to this goal?
12. How open to constructive criticism are you? What could you do to improve your openness to criticism?
13. How much could you have contributed to the problem?
14. How much do you respect your colleagues? Yourself?
15. How much is enough/good enough?
16. How much of your work is challenging intellectually?
17. How much/often is enough?
18. How pure are your intentions?
19. How will you feel about this decision when you look back at it in 2 years' time?
20. How will you make it possible to hear those unwelcome messages?
21. How would [role model] handle this?
22. How would you explain this to your children/partner/family?
23. How/what do you feel?
24. I don't know what to do about that; what do you think?
25. If all the obstacles disappeared, what would you do?
26. If our roles were reversed, what would you be asking me right now?
27. If this is really what you want to do, why haven't you started?
28. If this issue were an animal/car, can you describe what would it be like?
29. If you did know the answer, what would it be?
30. If you get that outcome will that give you what you want?
31. If you had another 100 years to live, would this still be a priority for you?
32. If you had only 6 months to live, would this still be a priority for you?
33. If you were independently wealthy, would you still come to work? So what is it that your work gives you over and above money? Could you get that another way?
34. If you weren't here for a month, what wouldn't get done?
35. If your direct reports could really say what they think, without fear of offending, what might they tell you?
36. Is it more important to you to be right rather than respected? Liked rather than efficient? Understood rather than understanding?
37. What are your beliefs around this issue? Which are helpful and which unhelpful?
38. What are your responsibilities here?

39. What could increase your commitment?
40. What could you do to obtain timelier, more constructive feedback?
41. What could you stop doing that would help your situation?
42. What do you care about?
43. What do you fear most?
44. What do you notice about your part in this?
45. What do you resent most about…?
46. What do you think you might be doing that would cause other people to fear/mistrust/resent you?
47. What do you want people to say about you at your funeral?
48. What do you want the outcome to be?
49. What do you want to be remembered for?
50. What do you want to become?
51. What do you/could you do to show that you care?
52. What does this mean for you?
53. What does this situation/experience tell you about yourself?
54. What does your gut instinct tell you?
55. What else could you do?
56. What else have you done?
57. What first steps could you take that would give you the confidence to make real progress?
58. What happens if you do nothing?
59. What have you not done?
60. What help do you want/would you most value from me?
61. What is the quick-fix solution? The permanent solution? What are the pluses and minuses of each?
62. What is your *need* from this situation?
63. What is your purpose? (either general – What are you on earth for?; or specific, about this issue)
64. What kind of role model do you think you represent here? What kind do you *want* to present?
65. What makes you feel valued?
66. What makes you get out of bed in the morning? What makes you think you'd rather stay there?
67. What messages do you not want to hear?
68. What need are you addressing when you behave in this way?
69. What permission have you given [other person]? Yourself?
70. What stops you walking away?
71. What two or three things would make a difference to how you feel, if you focused on doing them and ignored everything else?
72. What unintended messages might you be sending in this situation?
73. What was your part in that?

74. What were the differences between the best and worst (career) decisions you have made?
75. What will/could you lose by winning?
76. What would a fly on the wall say was going on?
77. What would be the impact of doing exactly the opposite of what is planned?
78. What would put you back in control?
79. What would the other party see you doing?
80. What would you ask yourself if you were me?
81. What would you have liked the other person to say? Why didn't they?
82. What would you liked to have said? What stopped you?
83. What would your best-self say or do here?
84. What's stopping you facing up to this? (Less confrontive than 'Why don't you?')
85. What's the consequence of not doing that?
86. What's the danger here?
87. What's your greatest ambition?
88. What's your greatest fear?
89. When your future self looks back at this, what should you have learned from it?
90. Where's the enjoyment in what you do?
91. Who are you? Who do you want to be?
92. Who could/should you ask for help? What's stopping you doing so?
93. Who do you compare yourself with? Who would you like to compare yourself with? Why?
94. Who do you need to give you permission to do this? What's stopping you giving yourself permission?
95. Who do you want to be?
96. Who else exerts control on your decisions?
97. Who else has call upon your time, your mental energy, your attention?
98. Who else shares ownership of this issue with you?
99. Who else's job are you doing as well as your own?
100. Who is in control of this situation?
101. Who knows? Who can? Who will?
102. Who owns your time?
103. Whose opinion do you value?
104. Why do you think people say/think that about you?
105. Why does this matter?
106. Why might that not be the right way forward?
107. *And finally, the one that does pretty well everything that you need:* Wassup?

Focus on the learner

Whatever questions we ask, it is useful to notice how we phrase them. Do our questions suggest that the player is responding so as to inform us of the situation so that we can be better able to take wise action? Or is our approach to help learners come to their own sense of the situation? Do we say:

- Describe to me…
- What you told me…

… which are focused upon us getting the information?
Or do we ask:

- What would you like to say about…?
- What do you want to look at…?

… which maximize the learner's choice?

Up and down the ladder

When we are working with a mentee, we often follow the line of their interest, and the conversation develops from what they say. We also influence the direction by choosing particular aspects of their comments to pick up on.

Make a note of the questions you ask in a mentoring or coaching session and, briefly, the responses of your learner. After 10 minutes or so, suggest to the learner that you stop to review where the conversation has gone and where it could most usefully go for them next.

Pursue this direction, and stop after another 10 minutes and check again. The learner may want to continue and perhaps deepen the direction that you have taken or it may be time to branch out again. Get into the habit of introducing this option as a regular part of letting your learner determine the direction of the conversation.

Remember that questions, particularly probing questions, do not leave the mentee wholly in command. In fact, if over-used they can become like interrogation.

Fix the learning

Before crystallizing a technique it is as well to be clear what kind of learning emerges from its use. This is important in the development of our learners – as in the case study of Ivana.

Case study   **Ivana coached by Rashmi**

A coach, Rashmi, did a highly effective piece of work with Ivana, a finance officer, who was famously aggressive in the company. Rashmi helped Ivana to develop a strategy with two senior people who were her internal clients and who resented her style. Ivana succeeded in bringing the two senior managers round and was delighted.

Sometime later Ivana was devastated when she got a similar, resentful reaction from another senior manager in the company. She experienced the repeated problem as doubly damaging as she thought that she had dealt with this issue and could move forward with confidence and joy.

Rashmi realized that a mistake had been made in not fixing the learning. Focusing on that would have helped Ivana realize that if it happened again, she shouldn't be surprised – we don't change that deeply. However, neither need Ivana be dismayed, because she has enlarged her repertoire to deal with such eventualities.

Reference

Megginson, D. (1999). *Creating Intellectual Properties: A Sensemaking Study.* Unpublished Doctoral Thesis at Lancaster University Management School.

Part 3

Where to From Here?

In the final part of this book we offer a guide to the other sources of information about coaching and mentoring that you may find useful in developing your skills and experience.

A. Resources

There are many books and packages that touch upon aspects of the ground covered here and, of course, go into great depth in areas that we only mention in passing. We have listed our top fifteen sources and have written a paragraph about each so that if you are unfamiliar with it you will gain some idea of whether it would be worth adding to your own library of resources. We have focused upon books rather than resource packs because of their relative value for money and therefore their accessibility to a wider population.

Alred, G., Garvey, B. and Smith, R. (1998). *The Mentoring Pocketbook*. Alresford, Hants: Management Pocketbooks.
A small, handout-sized booklet offering sound advice and a 3-stage process for mentoring.

Bast, M. and Thomson, C. (2003). *Out of the Box: Coaching with the Enneagram*. Portland, Oregon: Stellar Attractions.
An alternative personality model to Myers Briggs (see Hirsh and Kise below) with its implications worked out for coaching.

Caplan, J. (2003). *Coaching for the Future: How Smart Companies Use Coaching and Mentoring*. London: CIPD.
Puts coaching in the context of organization culture, management style and other training interventions.

Clutterbuck, D. (2004). *Everyone Needs a Mentor*, 4th edn. London: CIPD.
The classic text on mentoring. Has much on setting up schemes as well as advice on techniques and approaches to mentoring.

Clutterbuck, D. and Megginson, D. (1999). *Mentoring Executives and Directors*. Oxford: Butterworth-Heinemann.
Through a string of case studies of executive mentoring, shows a range of techniques and approaches, which are pulled together in a final section.

Clutterbuck, D. and Ragins, B. R. (2002). *Mentoring and Diversity: An International Perspective*. Oxford: Butterworth-Heinemann.
Full of techniques and frameworks for mentoring in an area that is taking on increasing importance.

Colley, H. (2003). *Mentoring for Social Inclusion: A Critical Approach to Nurturing Mentor Relationships*. London: RoutledgeFalmer.
Focuses on youth mentoring, conceptually rigorous analysis of resistance and agency; surveillance and transformation; empowerment and control.

Downey, M. (2004). *Effective Coaching*, 2nd edn. London: Texere.
A greatly extended and improved second edition, which makes the case for a thorough-going learner-directed approach.

Hirsh, S. A. and Kise, J. A. G. (2000). *Introduction to Type and Coaching*. Palo Alto, CA: Consulting Psychologists Press.
For those familiar with the Myers Briggs personality preference framework, this booklet spells out the coaching implications, offering generic tools and details of how each of the 16 types function, contribute and respond to stress. They outline the areas in which each type may need coaching and spell out how they would like to be coached.

Landsberg, M. (2003). *The Tao of Coaching*. London: Profile.
A small book, full of cartoons, pragmatic examples and wisdom.

Lee, G. (2003). *Leadership Coaching*. London: CIPD.
An accessible psychodynamic approach to executive coaching. Advocates coaching for authentic leadership and includes critiques of defiant and compliant behaviour.

McLeod, A. (2003). *Performance Coaching: A Handbook for Managers, H R Professionals and Coaches*. Bancyfelin, Carmarthen: Crown House.
Of the great number of NLP-influenced handbooks that we have read, this has the clearest insights into the strengths and limitations of the approach.

Rosinski, P. (2003). *Coaching across Cultures: New Tools for Leveraging National, Corporate and Professional Differences*. London: Nicholas Brealey.
Using a framework of dimensions of national culture, issues in cross-cultural leadership coaching are elucidated and tools are described.

Shaw, P. (2002). *Changing Conversations in Organisations: A Complexity Approach to Change*. London: Routlege.
Avoiding simple nostrums and two-by-two matrices, this book explores uncertainty and complexity, advocating acting with intention into the unknowable. Rigorous and at the same time explicit, with detailed accounts of conversations about change.

Whitmore, J. (2003). *Coaching for Performance: GROWing People, Performance and Purpose*, 3rd edn. London: Nicholas Brealey.
Clear, simple, principled. An outline of the GROW framework for performance improvement and including useful explorations of purpose and meaning in coaching.

B. Organizations

The following are organizations that have a contribution to make to the field and may provide readers with membership benefits.

The Association for Coaching (www.associationforcoaching.com) sees itself as promoting excellence and ethics in coaching. It has both individual and provider organization members. It has a Code of Ethics and Good Practice and a Complaints Procedure, and offers qualified members a certificate.

The Coaching and Mentoring Network (www.coachingnetwork.org.uk) is a UK-focused web-based network offering subscribers free impartial information about referrals (it charges coaches to register) and resources. It offers software and Internet development services, a coach matching service, and does not accredit its members.

The Coaching Psychology Forum (www.coachingpsychologyforum.org. uk) was founded in 2002 in response to concern about untrained or poorly trained coaches and the need to promote improved standards of practice. In 2004 the CPF had 400 members and affiliate members from within the British Psychological Society, more than 75 per cent of whom were chartered members.

The European Mentoring and Coaching Council (www.emccouncil.org) arose out of the European Mentoring Centre that was founded in 1992. It exists to promote good practice in mentoring and coaching across Europe. By 2004 it had developed and applied a widely agreed Code of Ethics in coaching and mentoring and Guidelines on Supervision, a Diversity Policy and a Complaints Procedure. It was bringing to a conclusion a wide-ranging project to identify common competences as a basis for agreeing a set of professional standards for both coaching and mentoring. It produced a similar set of standards for mentoring schemes. It has established an electronic professional and academic journal, *The International Journal for Mentoring and Coaching*, and holds a major conference each year. EMCC is growing fast and in 2004 had more than 250 individual members and more than 25 organizational members.

The International Coach Federation (www.coachfederation.org) describes itself as the professional association of personal and business coaches that seeks to preserve the integrity of coaching around the globe. It is a US-based individual membership international organization with more than 6000 members and 145 chapters in more than 30 countries. It has developed a Code of Ethics and of Professional Standards, offers a Coach Referral Service and has a system for accrediting members. It holds an annual conference.

The National Mentoring Network (www.nmn.org.uk) was founded in 1994 and mainly focuses on mentoring schemes in schools. It aims to promote the development of mentoring and quality standards; to offer advice and support to those developing mentoring programmes; and to exchange information on good practice. It has 1500 organization members and 400 individual mentor members. It has an annual conference, a library, regional networks and a scheme-accreditation process leading to Approved Provider Standard. NMN founded, in 1998, the UK Mentoring Strategy Group to influence mentoring across the UK.

C. Means of deepening your skills and knowledge

There is an increasing number of sources and courses to develop skill and knowledge about coaching and mentoring. As things are changing so rapidly, we offer basic details about the orientations and approach of each rather than evaluating them, which we leave to the cautious buyer.

Masters Degree programmes

i-coach academy (accredited by *Middlesex University*) runs a post-graduate Certificate and a professional Masters degree (both part-time). The Certificate year focuses on participants identifying their own model for coaching; the Masters year produces critiques of these models using a multiplicity of frameworks. The related *International Centre for the Study of Coaching* (also accredited by *Middlesex University*) runs a professional Doctoral programme in a number of centres throughout the world.

Oxford Brookes University. Embedded in the Education Faculty of the university, this was the first Masters programme to be offered in the UK. Some participants of the OSCM (see below) courses move on to the Oxford Brookes course, carrying a modest credit of M-level points.

Sheffield Hallam University. Linked to a suite of programmes in change and consultancy, this programme has both the authors of this book involved in its delivery, so it would be invidious to comment further.

Wolverhampton University. The newest programme that we have found on coaching in a UK university.

Other qualification courses

Academy of Executive Coaching offers a master coach development programme and an MSc degree accredited by *Middlesex University*. The programme has an interesting Gestalt therapy orientation.

Chartered Institute of Personnel and Development. CIPD's commercial arm, CIPD Services, offer a (200 learning hours) largely e-delivered Certificate in Coaching and Mentoring (Vocational Qualification level 3) which leads to Associate Membership of CIPD. It has recruited 300 participants in the first 3 years of operation. It also organizes a one-day conference annually. The Membership and Education side of CIPD was in 2004 considering developing standards at Masters level. Its Professional Knowledge Department produced, in June 2004, a Guide to Coaching and Mentoring.

Oxford School of Coaching and Mentoring. Offers a CIPD programme as well as its own certificate which leads into the Masters programme at Oxford Brookes University.

References

Anderson, W. (1996). *The Face of Glory: Creativity, Consciousness and Civilization*. London: Bloomsbury.

Argyris, C. (1991). Teaching smart people how to learn. *Harvard Business Review*, May–June, 99–109.

Bandler, R. and Grinder, J. (1975). *The Structure of Magic*. Palo Alto: Science & Behavior Books.

Bast, M. and Thomson, C. (2003). *Out of the Box: Coaching with the Enneagram*. Portland, Oregon: Stellar Attractions.

Berne, E. (1975). *What Do You Say After You Say Hello?* London: Corgi/Transworld.

Bettelheim, B. (1991). *The Uses of Enchantment*. London: Penguin.

Bolton, G. (2001). *Reflective Practice: Writing and Professional Development*. London: Paul Chapman.

Bolton, G., Howlett, S., Lago, C. and Wright, J. K. (2004). *Writing Cures: An Introductory Handbook of Writing in Counselling and Psychotherapy*. Hove: Brunner-Routledge.

Boyatzis, R., Howard, A., Kapisara, B. and Taylor, S. (2004). Target practice. *People Management*, 11 March, 26–32.

Bridger, H. (1990). Courses and working conferences as transitional learning institutions. In *The Social Engagement of Social Science, Vol. 1, The Socio-Psychological Perspective* (Trist, E. and Murray, H. eds). Free Associations Books.

Bruch, B. and Ghoshal, S. (2002). Beware the busy manager. *Harvard Business Review*, **80**(2), 62–69.

Bruner, J. (1990). *Acts of Meaning*. London: Harvard University Press.

Buzan, T. (1995). *Use your Head*. London: BBC Books.

Canfield, J., Hansen, M. V. and Hewitt, L. (2000). *The Power of Focus*. Deerfield Beach, Fl: Health Communications.

Clutterbuck, D. (1998). *Learning Alliances*. London: CIPD.

Clutterbuck, D. and Megginson, D. (1999). *Mentoring Executives and Directors*. Oxford: Butterworth-Heinemann.

Clutterbuck, D. and Megginson, D. (2004). All good things must come to an end: winding up and winding down a mentoring relationship. In *The Situational Mentor* (Clutterbuck, D. and Lane, G., eds). Aldershot: Gower.

Clutterbuck, D. and Ragins, B. R. (2002). *Mentoring and Diversity*. Oxford: Butterworth-Heinemann.

De Bono, E. (1990). *Six Thinking Hats*. Harmondsworth: Penguin.

Donnison, P. A. (2000), *Images of Outdoor Management Development. A Synthesis of the Literature and Participants' Experiences on Outdoor Courses*. PhD dissertation, Department of Management Learning, Lancaster University.

Downey, M. (2004). *Effective Coaching* 2nd edn. London: Texere.

Doyle, B. and O'Neill, V. (2001). *Mentoring Entrepreneurs*. Cork: Oak Tree Press.

English, P. (2004). *Succeeding at Interviews Pocketbook*. Alresford: Management Pocketbooks.

Farrelly, F. and Bradsma, J. (1974). *Provocative Therapy*. Cupertino, CA: Meta Publications.

Fordham, F. (1991). *An Introduction to Jung's Psychology*. Harmondsworth: Penguin.

Grayling, A. C. (2004). *What is Good?* London: Orion.

Greene, J. and Grant, A. (2001). *Solution-focused Coaching: Managing People in a Complex World*. London: Momentum.

Hirsh, S. A. and Kise, J. A. G. (2000). *Introduction to Type and Coaching*. Palo Alto, CA: Consulting Psychologists, Press.

Kelly, G. A. (1955). *The Psychology of Personal Constructs*, Vols 1 and 2. New York: W W Norton.

Landsberg, M. (1996). *The Tao of Coaching*. London: Harper Collins.

Lee, G. (2003). *Leadership Coaching*. London: CIPD.

Local Government Management Board/Institute of Local Government Studies (1991). *Quality and Equality: Service to the Whole Community*. Birmingham: Birmingham University.

Maslow, A. (1954). *Motivation and Personality*. New York: Harper & Row.

McAdams, D. P. (1993). *The Stories We Live By*. New York and London: Guilford Press.

McDermott, I. and Jago, W. (2001). *The NLP Coach*. London: Piatkus.

McLeod, A. (2003). *Performance Coaching: A Handbook for Managers, H. R. Professionals and Coaches*. Bancyfelin, Carmarthen: Crown House.

Megginson, D. (1999). *Creating Intellectual Properties: A Sensemaking Study*. Unpublished Doctoral Thesis at Lancaster University Management School.

Megginson, D. (2000). Current issues in mentoring. *Career Development International*, **5**(4–5), 256–60.

Megginson, D. and Whitaker, V. (2003). *Continuing Professional Development*. London: CIPD.

Murray, W. H. (2002). *The Evidence of Things not Seen: A Mountaineer's Tale*. London: Bâton Wicks.

Perls, F. (1971). *Gestalt Therapy Verbatim*. New York: Bantam.

Persaud, R. (2001). *Staying Sane: How to Make Your Mind Work for You*. London: Bantam.

Revans, R. (1998). *The ABC of Action Learning*. London: Lemos & Crane.

Rosinski, P. (2003). *Coaching Across Cultures*. London: Nicholas Brealey.

Srivastva, S. and Cooperrider, D. L. (eds) (1990) *Appreciative Management and Leadership: The Power of Positive Thought and Action in Organizations*. San Francisco: Jossey-Bass.

Vince, R. and Martin, L. (1993). Inside action learning: an exploration of the psychology and politics of the action learning model. In *Management Education and Development*, **24**(3), 205–15.

Watson, T. (1996). 'Motivation: that's Maslow, isn't it?' *Management Learning*, **27**(4), 447–64.

Weick, K. E. (1995). *Sensemaking in Organisations*. London: Sage.

Whitmore, J. (2003). *Coaching for Performance: GROWing People, Performance and Purpose*, 3rd edn. London: Nicholas Brealey.

Whitworth, L., Kimsey House, H. and Sandhal, P. (1998). *Co-Active Coaching*. Palo Alto, CA: Davies-Black.

Yerkes, R. M. and Dodson, J. D. (1908). The relative strength of stimulus to rapidity of habit formation. *Journal of Comparative Neurology and Psychology*, **18**, 459–82.

Index